Everyday
Dog

This lovely little Shetland Sheepdog teen exemplifies the "everyday dog." Her owner's pet, she received her first two championship points from the puppy class; she is getting ready for her obedience CD; she has already passed a herding instinct test; and she is a whiz at agility!

Everyday Dog

Training Your Dog
to Be the Companion You Want

Nancy E. Johnson

HOWELL
BOOK HOUSE

New York

MAXWELL MACMILLAN INTERNATIONAL
NEW YORK   OXFORD   SINGAPORE   SYDNEY

Howell Book House
Macmillan Publishing Company
866 Third Avenue, New York, NY 10022

Collier Macmillan Canada, Inc.
1200 Eglinton Avenue East, Suite 200
Don Mills, Ontario M3C 3N1

Library of Congress Cataloging-in-Publication Data

Johnson, Nancy E., 1939–
    Everyday dog/Nancy E. Johnson.
        p.   cm.
    Summary: A guide to daily care of a dog, including toilet
training, socialization, and obedience.
        ISBN 0-87605-544-7
    1. Dogs—Training.   2. Dogs—Showing.   [1. Dogs—Training.]
    I. Title.
    SF431.J64   1990
    636.7′0887—dc20   89-77767   CIP

Macmillan books are available at special discounts for bulk purchases for sales promotions, premiums, fund-raising, or educational use. For details contact:

                        Special Sales Director
                        Macmillan Publishing Company
                        866 Third Avenue
                        New York, NY 10022

10 9 8 7 6 5 4 3 2 1

Printed in the United States of America

Dedicated to my parents, Al and Ellen Sonneman, no longer here, but ever present; to my sons, David and John Klinkerman, of whom I cannot speak highly enough; and, to my friend, Jean Towner, whose morning wake-up calls allow a measure of continuity to my life.

This Labrador Retriever puppy is getting an early jump on its life's work.

Contents

Picture Acknowledgments

My thanks to—

Dog	Breed	Owner
Abby	Newfoundland	Pat Meadows
Whitney	Dalmatian	Dave, Sue and Travis Geisler
Solo	Samoyed	Emily Krozak
Xorah	German Shepherd Dog	Bart and Shirley Levy
Benny	Basenji	Mickey Rubin
Penny	Australian shepherd mix	Kathy Oleson
Lady, CDX	American Eskimo	Kathy Butler
Rowdy	American Eskimo	Kathy Butler
Ch. Connor	Irish Setter	Elyse Hansberry
Ch. Cacia, UDTX, JH, WCX	Golden Retriever	Jeanne von Barby
Vanna	Labrador Retriever	Mike Diefendorfer
Tori	Doberman Pinscher	Dorothy Foegen
Shire	Doberman Pinscher	Dorothy Foegen
Cessie, UD	Samoyed	Mary Powell
Bubba	Chinese Shar Pei	Karla Lewis

Dog	Breed	Owner
Sugar	Shetland Sheepdog	Chris Menely
Sophie	Australian	Zo Miller
Janelle	Shetland Sheepdog	Beverly Muhlenhaupt
Phoenix	Siberian Husky	Larry Houser
Saki	Akita	Ray Rosenburg
Ambassador	Akita	Shirley A. Rollins
Ch. Casey, CDX, TDX	Pembroke Welsh Corgi	Carole-Joy Evert
Tabby, CDX	Australian Terrier	Cathy Lester
Bonnie, CDX	Bernese Mountain Dog	Mary Weight
Mitsy	German Shepherd Dog	Monica Priller
Caleb	Rottweiler	Shelley Voorhees
Ch. Remus, UDTDX	Rottweiler	Shelley Voorhees
Twinkle	Keeshond	Jennifer Prescott-Downing
Spirit	Rottweiler	Shelley Voorhees
Heather	Doberman Pinscher	Nancy Jewell
Favor	Tibetan Spaniel	Kay Dickenson
Zach	Belgian Tervuren	Nick Yeanopolis
Holly	Shetland Sheepdog	Jean Towner and Nancy Johnson
Sophie	Australian shepherd mix	Zo Miller
Chloe	Bichon Frise	Donna Rogers
Otch Debbie	Shetland Sheepdog	Richard Cook
Odie, Crackers	Labrador Retrievers	Charlotte Hart
Mandy, CDX	American Cocker Spaniel	Suzette Compton
Toby, CDX	Basset Hound	Nicole Turner
File Photo	Scottish Deerhound	Mickey Rubin, photographer
Teddy	Shetland Sheepdog	Janet Harris
San	Miniature Pinscher	Ila Dombowsky
Topper, UD	Shetland Sheepdog	Nancy Johnson
Ch. Rage, CDX	Doberman Pinscher	Janet Harris

Introduction

AFTER thirty-five years of training dogs, I find that the questions I am asked by new dog owners and by people who have never "trained" their dogs remain the same. This book attempts to answer those questions by suggesting positive solutions.

People come from all walks of life, and so do dogs. Some dogs are born with years of planning behind their debut; some are born because of an open gate!

Just as all people must adapt to the basic rules of the society in which they live, so must all dogs. It makes no difference if your job at the FAA is to head it or to sweep the runways it supervises, you still have to pass through a metal detector on the way to the plane. And it makes no difference if your new puppy is being trained for Madison Square Garden or to help your child deliver the newspapers; he still has to be housebroken and he still must not bite the mailman!

Whatever your lifestyle, and whatever type of dog you choose, this book allows you to introduce your new puppy to your way of living, using sound principles right from the start. The book teaches you how to teach basic house and street manners according to what is important to you. It offers a look at some wonderful sports available to you and your dog. For those who are competitive, it shows you how to give your puppies the outlook they need for a successful career. It lets you have the fun of teaching your dog the tricks you see other dogs perform in movies and commercials, while at the same time instilling positive social behavior and modifying submissive or aggressive behavior.

This book gives you the ability to rear a wonderful pet and serviceable companion through simple techniques. Its basic guidelines enable you to teach your puppy to learn *positively* so that whatever job you choose for him, he will be a socially acceptable animal.

Most people's lives are filled with a variety of work and play; your dog's life can be, too. Your everyday dog can win Best in Show, deliver papers, complete a Utility degree, hunt with Dad in the field, run a lure course, pull a sled or participate in whatever type of activity his heritage allows him, as well as bring you your slippers at night! Only your ability to teach him will limit what he can learn. And the more he knows, the more useful and cherished he will become.

This book will make it possible for you to choose what you want your puppy to learn—or, if you have chosen an adult dog to come into your home, to recondition and redirect him so he may become the dog you thought you bought! If you follow the guidelines faithfully for just a few months, the lessons learned will last your everyday dog a lifetime.

Please note: Gender in this book is expressed in male terminology. It is simply easier than to distinguish between man and woman, girl and boy, dog and bitch, him and her or the dreaded "it." Just think of our everyday person or everyday dog as being whatever gender pleases you. Take no offense, for none is meant.

Terminology

BAIT: A treat used to get your dog to give you his attention.

COLLARS: A "puppy" collar is a buckle collar made from a wide piece of cotton or nylon fabric. A slip or chain "choke" collar is made from cotton, nylon or chain. The best chain collars are brass with very tight, small links.

CORD or LONG-LINE: A piece of cotton or nylon cord, very lightweight and small in diameter (in relation to the size of your puppy or dog) with a snap at one end and a handle at the other.

CORRECTION: A physical or verbal restraint to the dog.

FREE: Without restraint.

LEASH/LEAD: A leash is a six-foot leather line with a handle at one end and a snap at the other. It should be small enough in width to comfortably fit in your hand.

PRAISE: Positive physical or verbal reassurance to reward your dog.

REWARD: An edible treat or tossable toy.

SHOW LEASH/LEAD: A lightweight lead. This leash comes in different materials, fabrics and lengths. Some show leashes have collars built in; some are to be attached to separate collars.

VETERINARIAN: A man who knows how important your dog is to you and who will answer you anytime you need him; a man you like, respect, will follow orders from and to whom you will pay bills promptly!

1

Introducing the Puppy to Your Way of Living

W HEN CONSIDERING what you feel are good manners for your puppy, imagine him not as a puppy, but as a fully grown, adult dog. Puppies are only puppies for a short time—probably eight to eighteen months, depending on the breed you have chosen. Whatever you consider acceptable for the puppy, you must also consider acceptable for the adult. A five-pound puppy is cute and cuddly in your lap—but is a 120-pound dog? A five-pound puppy may look cute carrying around your slipper, but how cute is a 120-pound dog that has just destroyed your ninety-dollar shoes! Just remember: What the puppy learns, the adult remembers.

This does not mean you must raise your puppy with an iron hand. On the contrary, I recommend just the opposite. By rearing him with gentle techniques that give positive guidelines, you both can enjoy the conditioning that will enable him to become socially acceptable.

Lay out schedules and rules from the start, with patience, persistence and praise beginning on the first day of the puppy's arrival. As you choose among the following guidelines, remember that consistency is necessary for success!

GUIDELINES

Housebreaking

Housebreaking is always uppermost in everyone's mind. It is simply done by:

1. Feeding the puppy at the same times every day.
2. Taking him outside *as soon as* he turns his head away from the food bowl and keeping him outside until he has urinated and defecated.
3. Taking him back inside and playing with him for a little while, then either—
4. Tying him *to you* on an eight- to ten-foot lightweight cord or putting him in his playpen or crate until you can watch him again.
5. Taking him outside between feedings *each* time and *as soon as* he wakes and *every time* he starts getting restless in the box or starts pulling at the end of his cord and looking uncomfortable.
6. Taking the puppy to the same area each time you take him outside and *telling* him what you want: "Go potty." (That way, when he is older and you want to leave him for some time or take him somewhere and be sure he will not embarrass you, you can "make him" eliminate when you want him to eliminate.)

Sleeping Through the Night

The first nights in a new home for a puppy are much like a baby's first few nights at home. The best way to get the puppy to sleep through the night quietly is to:

1. Make sure his last play period is a good, hearty one that *ends* about one hour before you feed him his last meal, which should be about an hour before *your* bedtime.
2. Take him out to potty as soon as he is done eating and about fifteen minutes before you go to bed.
3. Leave a very small quantity of water with him when you put him to bed.
4. Try to make your bedtime and his getting-up time no more than six hours

Bedtime Schedule

7:30 P.M.–8:00 P.M.	Play period—hard
8:00 P.M.–9:00 P.M.	Play period—quiet
9:00 P.M.	Feeding
9:10 P.M.	Potty
9:50 P.M.	Potty
10:00 P.M.	Bedtime

By tying your puppy to you, you can get your work done and he will stay out of trouble.

Your puppy's bed can be a rug at the end of your bed, a box or crate or pen or any other small area that restricts his movement.

apart until he is four to five months old. With this schedule—and proper containment—a healthy puppy should both sleep and housebreak easily.

5. Make him a proper bed. The puppy's "bed" can be a rug at the end of your bed (tie him to the bedpost), a box or crate or pen, or any other small area that restricts his movement. You want him sleeping while you are sleeping!

Crate or Pen Training

Crate or pen training is easy as long as you know a puppy's nature and follow his physiological rules. Dogs have always been bred to have enough energy to do something—pull, hunt, herd, guard and so forth. They have been given lots of energy to accomplish those jobs and they must do something with that energy. As long as *you* direct how your puppy uses that energy, he will readily adjust to crate or pen training. Try adapting the following type of schedule into your daily schedule.

1. Let your puppy burn off his immediate energy by running free (in an enclosed, supervised area) for ten to twenty minutes to get the "silliness" out.
2. Burn off the reserve energy by giving him something to do that will both use his mind and serve your future purposes, such as:

   - fetch his favorite toy (1,000 times!)
   - run through the KPT agility course (pp. 29–32)
   - play hide and seek (pp. 27–29)
   - any other energy-using positive activity you both enjoy.

3. Leave the puppy alone for about fifteen minutes after he tires and prepare his meal.
4. Feed him (in his crate if you wish) and then let him out to potty.
5. Crate or pen him for an hour. (Ignore any initial pleading for release.)
6. Repeat the procedure at least once a day for the first three months you have him at home. The crate can become his den if you wish and is a safe place for you to leave him for short periods of time.

Submissive Urination

Submissive urination is frustrating for both you and the puppy. Several things need to be considered, but usually the treatment is very easy to administer and very effective. First, check with your veterinarian to be sure there are no urological problems, nor an infection that would either cause or contribute to frequent urination. Once health problems are eliminated, follow the guidelines below and make sure everyone else—family members, guests and strangers—follows them, too.

1. Do not bend over the dog. Always let him come up to you and reach up to you for a pat.

4

2. Do not look down at the dog, but look slightly away as you pat him, until he gains more security. Help him gain that security by *eye contact* (see the following section).
3. If you want the dog, sit down near him with your back to him. Munch on something until he comes up to see what you have, or play with a soft stuffed toy until you gain his interest. When he comes, give him a piece of your food or let him have the toy and quietly clip the leash or cord to his collar. Give him a pat and a "Good boy"; attach him to you and go about your business.
4. Whenever anyone else comes into the room, have him *ignore* the puppy and talk to you. Sit on chairs or couches and when the puppy wants attention, make sure he receives none until his head and body come *up* to your hand. Do not reach down to him. Continue to avoid all eye contact until the puppy quits squirming when you give him attention.
5. As the puppy learns to accept eye contact, you may begin to approach him in a more conventional manner. Each step gained in confidence building will reduce the submissive urination. You must be patient and be sure *everyone* follows the same rules.

Eye Contact

Eye contact is best started with the puppy up on a table facing you. Be sure the table has stable footing (either a mat or rug) so the puppy will not slip.

1. Take his head in both of your hands by placing your fingertips under and around his cheeks, and support his bottom jaw with your palms and thumbs.
2. Gently raise his head and look directly into his eyes.
3. *As soon as* he gives you eye contact, quietly say "Good boy" and give him a treat, raising the treat just above his head before letting him eat it.
4. If he squirms and refuses to make eye contact, take a small piece of food and hold it between *your* eyes. When he looks at the food, wait until his eyes shift to yours, then give him the reward.
5. After the puppy accepts eye contact on the table, put him on the floor. Call him and tell him "Look" while you put the treat between your eyes. When he gives you eye contact, praise him and give him the treat.
6. Continue both the table work and the floor work until the puppy can give you his attention, immediately, without any problems.

Leash Breaking

Leash breaking is easily accomplished by placing a soft, wide, nylon buckle collar on the puppy. If you have a conformation puppy, be sure to follow Step 5 under this leash-breaking section.

Fear.

Curiosity.

Acceptance.

1. Put the collar on the puppy and attach it to a six-foot, lightweight, leather leash (one that fits comfortably in your hand).
2. Take some small chunks of hot dog, chicken or cheddar cheese, put them in a plastic sandwich bag and slip the bag into your pocket. Place the leash in your left hand and let it hang loosely down to the puppy at your left side. Put a piece of the treat in your right hand and put your right hand down close to the puppy's nose. Lead him forward with the food (like a donkey with a carrot). Be sure to keep your leash *loose*. Every few feet stop and give him a little piece of the treat and reward him with pats and praise.
3. Repeat the above steps six or seven times and then try the procedure without the food once or twice. If he comes along, praise him lavishly with your voice and pats. If he charges ahead, wait until he reaches the *end* of the leash, then snap him back and say (in a quiet, nonemotional voice) "No." If he dashes off again, repeat the snap and the "No." If he stops or comes back to you, praise him and give another treat. Be sure to speak softly to him when correcting. Your leash handles the correction. If you yell at him you will teach him to listen only when you yell!
4. Repeat this exercise three or four times a day, for just three or four minutes each time. Within a few days he will be leash broken (not "heeling," but not pulling either).
5. For conformation puppies, after your puppy walks alongside you for several paces, step in front of him, put both of your hands together—just in front of and above his head—and with the treat lead him toward you while you step backward. Stop after a few feet, give him a piece of the treat and raise your hands a few inches. When he stops chewing he will look to you for another treat. When he does, reward him. This little exercise instills "automatic ears" and "straight fronts" from the beginning and, if you intend to do both conformation and obedience, it will instill a standing free stack before the front sit is taught.

Jumping Up

A puppy's jumping on you is taken care of *without* kneeing the puppy (which can bruise his chest) or stepping on his toes (which can break soft puppy bones).

1. As the puppy jumps up, grasp him by his elbows (located along either side of his *chest*). Do not grasp his legs or feet. Walk *him* backward until he falls down. Turn and walk away.
2. Repeat this procedure every time the puppy jumps up.
3. Pat and praise every time your puppy comes to you and keeps all four feet on the ground.
4. Do not let young children try to back the puppy up. Invariably they grab the puppy by his legs and the puppy ends up biting the child, trying to get away.

Put the leash in your left hand and the bait in your right hand.

Gently coax the puppy to come along with you.

Be patient, be persistent and use plenty of praise!

Free baiting instills "automatic ears" and "straight fronts" from the very beginning.

Biting Children's Ankles

A puppy should not be biting children's ankles if you have the puppy tied to you on a cord. Remember, prevention is always the best way to keep bad habits from forming. If your puppy is not on a cord and he grabs at your child's ankles:

1. Put him on a cord and tie it to your waist.
2. Allow the puppy to get near the child and have the child run away.
3. As soon as the puppy makes *any* attempt to grab at the child's ankle, or any other part of his body, jerk the cord sharply and quietly say "No."
4. Have the child come back and have him *walk* away. Let the puppy follow along quietly. If he tries to grab, correct.
5. Repeat this combination of running and walking until the puppy shows no signs of wanting to grab at ankles (or jump on the child). Then let the child start running slowly and repeat the above steps as needed.
6. Make sure you take both your children and your puppy for long walks together. This teaches them to enjoy each other, with you in control. Encourage your child to throw sticks or investigate anything that can involve the puppy. In other words, teach them respect and tolerance for each other.

Biting Hands

Biting your hands is simply not allowed, nor is *leaning* against your body or *standing* on your feet. All these actions indicate either aggression or fear (real or "just testing") by your puppy. You want to teach the puppy to use his mouth for your benefit, so the correction must be clearly understood. There are many physical corrections that can be administered. Some of them work with some puppies, some with other puppies. But the danger in giving a physical correction is that all too often the person administering the correction does not have proper timing (or proper aim!), is too young to handle the situation properly or is not able to follow up on the correction properly. The situation just gets worse. A more positive and self-correcting method is to:

1. Get some fresh limes, cut in half and put them in the refrigerator before you bring the puppy home. The *very first time* your puppy mouths or bites your arm or hand, get the lime out!
2. Allow the puppy to mouth you again, then take the cut side of the lime in the hand on the arm that is not being mouthed, press the fresh lime against your puppy's nose, twist the lime (like squeezing an orange!), and quietly say "No." Make this a fairly long correction, as you want it to be quite unpleasant.
3. As soon as he backs off and licks his lips, stroke him gently from his shoulders back along his side and say "Good boy."

Grasp the puppy by his elbows and gently push him backward until he falls.

Oh, oh. Here I go.
She warned me not to jump.

11

Children should not be allowed to roughhouse with their pets. . .

. . . but should be taught to play with their dog in a positive manner.

12

Growing up without a fuss
　　Takes just a little care;
Time you'll spend in helping us
　　Will make a special pair!

Biting is totally unacceptable. The "lime-juice twist" is the perfect correction!

4. Repeat this every time the puppy mouths. It will not take more than a few times for him to learn that it is no fun to put your arm in his mouth!
5. Recognize that you should never encourage any games with puppies that will inadvertently teach them to try to dominate you physically. This includes tug-of-war, wrestling matches, and chase games. Substitute fetching or find-it games, agility or tracking for puppies, or any other energy-using game that is positive for the puppy yet lets you remain in control of the action. Roughhousing with a dog will encourage his aggressiveness and should only be used in teaching very submissive puppies to gain a measure of confidence, or with puppies whose owners know why they are allowing a certain amount of aggression. It is important that you and your children recognize the danger inappropriate games can pose.

Don't Chew That!

Your dog must be taught the following rule to live by: "Don't chew anything that I don't give you, and bring me everything else you put into your mouth!" Since, for the first few months of your new puppy's life, you are going to have him in a controlled area or on a line tied to your body, you will have complete control of what he can and cannot chew. Remember, if he learns as a puppy that he can chew on the hose, that is what he will do when you leave him alone and he gets bored.

1. Always play with his own toys. Throw them short distances and allow him to do whatever he wants to them (roll on them, chew on them, leave them alone or bring them back to you so you can throw them again).
2. Take him to an area of the house where you have planted something on the floor (a sock is always a good temptation). Sit within his reach of the item (be sure he is on the cord), and when he finds it and picks it up say, "Fetch, good! Fetch." *Gently* pull him to you with the cord (you want him to keep the sock in his mouth until he reaches you).
3. Take a treat out of your pocket and offer him the treat. He will drop the sock to get the treat. Praise him and take the sock.

"Fetch" can be used later for just about anything you want fetched (a soda from the refrigerator) and can be used to help you (put the empty can into the wastebasket), in obedience (fetch the dumbbell), in field work (fetch the bird) or in tricks (take this basket of mints and offer it to our guests). Remember, since you have control of the objects your puppy puts into his mouth, you do not have to *correct* him. You *want* him to learn to use his mouth in a way that benefits you!

Barking

Barking may be good or bad, depending on the occasion and your wishes. Use it to your advantage. Always go and see at what your dog is barking. It

I see you've noticed
The slipper I took
While you were reading
That dog training book.

But,
I guess if you'll follow
    Each tip and guideline
When I'm older I'll know
    It's yours and not mine!

16

is part of the dog's job, as our protector, to let us know when something is amiss. If you want him to keep barking, tell him "Speak, good boy, speak" until whatever he is barking at has gone. If you want to stop him from barking:

1. Look at whatever he is barking at for five seconds, then turn away and nonchalantly say, "It's okay. Quiet."
2. Calmly sit down and start reading a book or eating something. When the puppy gives you his attention and quits barking, give him a tidbit and a little pat, but not too much attention.
3. Stay seated for about five minutes, deliberately ignoring whatever is going on, then return to your chores. If it is not important to you, it will not be important to your puppy.

If your puppy is not one of the 99 percent that responds favorably to this behavior training—if he is hyperactive and does not really care about food—you can try two other exercises:

Spray bottle

1. Take a spray bottle filled with strong lime juice, walk to him and say, quietly, "Quiet."
2. Assuming he continues to bark, squirt the juice (lots of it!) directly into his mouth *until* he is quiet.
3. Repeat as often as he barks (even one bark) after you have told him to be quiet.

Rocks in a Plastic Bottle

1. Take a plastic bottle (Pepto-Bismol is a good one) and fill it about one-quarter full with small pebbles.
2. When the puppy starts barking say, quietly, "Quiet." If there is no response, throw the bottle at the space *behind* his tail (not at the puppy).
3. When he jumps up say "Good boy" and ignore him.
4. Repeat as needed.

Bothering You at Mealtime

Bothering at mealtime should not be allowed and is easily controlled.

1. Before sitting down to a meal, tie your puppy to a door, rail or chair—at whatever distance you wish, away from the table. If you want "his rug" there, fine.
2. Give him a small dog biscuit or chew bone.
3. Serve and enjoy your meal and *ignore* the puppy.
4. After four or five meals conducted in this manner, your puppy will realize that table food is not available to him, and he will lie quietly until you are finished.

5. If you wish to give table scraps to your puppy, save them and add *small* bits of them to his regular meal. That way he will not get overeager for you to end your meal, you will not feel guilty for "not giving him some" and your puppy will get proper nourishment by sticking mainly to his own food.

Scratching or Jumping on the Door

This may seem like a good way to allow the puppy to tell you when he wants in or out, but as he grows the scratching becomes more like clawing and for many obvious reasons is not a good idea. So, when teaching the puppy to ask to be let in or out, teach him to speak instead of scratch (p. 62). Then, when he understands "Speak":

1. When you know he needs to go out, take him to the door and tell him to speak. When he does, let him out.
2. When he comes back to the door to be let in, before you let him in, make him speak. When he does, let him in and praise him.

Climbing on Furniture

Climbing on furniture is okay for a puppy *if* you want your adult dog on your furniture. If you choose not to have the grown dog on your furniture, do not introduce the puppy to it at all (either on the furniture itself, or in your lap when you are sitting on the furniture). If he does get up there (without your help) make sure all your corrections are made without ever touching him.

1. Take hold of your cord about six feet from the puppy. Tell him "Off," and rather gently pop him off the furniture onto the floor.
2. As soon as he is on the floor—with all four feet—praise him with soft words and gentle strokes.
3. Sit down on the furniture and praise and pet him.

Digging

Digging is controlled by containment and by not allowing it to occur. Remember, everything your puppy learns when he is young is something he will retain and may revert to when he is older and either bored or frightened. Digging is particularly annoying to you but totally natural to the dog—so the two of you start with opposite viewpoints as to its desirability! As long as you are supervising the puppy properly for his first few months, he should have no opportunity to get his paws into the ground. However, if your puppy is out in the yard alone and you see him start to dig:

1. Leave him in the yard and get a good-sized bucket of ice-cold water.
2. Take it to the yard and wait until the puppy starts digging again. Walk

Digging is hard to control if your puppy yard is full of soft brush and fresh earth.

Proper use of the long line teaches your puppy respect for boundaries.

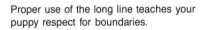

When he learns, he will wait until you tell him he can go in or out.

quietly over to him, quietly say "No" and dump the water from the bucket directly on top of the puppy.
3. Refill your bucket and wait for it to happen again. Repeat until the puppy walks away from the hole.

Running Out Gates and Doors

Allowing your dog to run out through a gate or door can be very dangerous. Again, control is the solution. First you must teach him what you want:

1. Have him sit (p. 39) at each door or gate you have that leads to an outside area and make him stay (pp. 43–44) there until you have gone through the door or gate.
2. Verbally give him permission to go through the opening.

When he has spent several days learning how to "wait" and you feel he has an idea of what you want, set up a correction.

1. Put him on a twenty-five-foot cord.
2. Leave the door or gate to the correction area open before allowing him in the correction area.
3. Walk into the area with the puppy and sit or stand twenty to twenty-five feet from the opening you have set up.
4. Wait until the puppy goes to the opening and puts the first foot through the opening.
5. Say "Stop," and from twenty to twenty-five feet away give the cord a good jerk. Turn and walk into another area (the cord will force the puppy to follow). When your puppy reaches you, praise and reward.
6. Repeat the correction until you see him going to the opening and sitting. You will have to reinforce this through the puberty stage!

Car Sickness

Car sickness affects more puppies emotionally than physically and can usually be easily cured.

1. Place the puppy in the car, *without* the car on or moving, for five minutes, then ten, then fifteen, waiting to increase the times at three-day intervals.
2. After nine days, repeat the exercise with the motor running but without the car moving.
3. After nine more days, drive for a few blocks and then turn around—slowly—and drive back. Repeat for nine more days.
4. Start short normal trips.

Car rowdiness is best controlled with a crate.

Car Rowdiness

Car rowdiness is dangerous for everyone concerned and is simply controlled either by crating the dog or by shutting the leash into the car door about two feet from where it is attached to the puppy. This permits enough leash room for the dog to sit, stand or lie down, but not enough for him to jump around.

Introducing Puppy to Established Pets

Introducing a puppy to the existing pets in a household is accomplished positively if the established housepet(s) is (are) acknowledged *before* the puppy is acknowledged.

1. Before bringing puppy home, feed your established pet a partial meal.
2. When you bring the puppy home, bring your pet outside to greet the puppy. If you have a particularly dominant-type pet, arrange this meeting a block or so from your home.
3. Walk the pet with the puppy (however well you can get the puppy to walk!) and let the existing pet sniff the puppy all he wants. Stay outside for forty-five minutes to an hour.
4. Take the pet and puppy into the house and just walk around the house for ten to fifteen minutes, letting everyone get adjusted to a new body in the house.
5. Feed the established pet another partial meal and let puppy *watch.*
6. Feed the established pet again, and this time put a bowl down for puppy. If the other pet comes to the puppy's bowl, tell him "No." Whenever you feed your animals, feed the older ones first, but make them respect the puppy's bowl.

Socialization with Friends

Socialization with friends should always be started on a positive yet controlled basis, as you want the puppy happy and unafraid—and your friends free of muddy paws and unscratched by sharp toenails.

When friends come into your home:

1. Keep puppy on a leash to prevent jumping.
2. Make sure your friends *first* talk with you for several minutes *before* speaking to the puppy. This gives the puppy time to sniff and relax a little.
3. Have your friends sit down with you and greet the puppy quietly and casually, in a friendly but not overpowering manner, by speaking to him and stroking him gently.

A young Belgian Tervuren says hello to a slightly older Shetland Sheepdog.

Remember, if your friends greet the puppy too enthusiastically, that is how he will greet them!

When you meet friends on the street:

1. Keep your puppy quiet by first talking with your friends and not acknowledging the puppy.
2. Let puppy sniff and relax.
3. Have your friends offer gentle words and quiet stroking.
4. Walk with the friends for a few minutes.
5. Have your friends take the puppy's leash for a few minutes, then switch it back to you.

Socialization with Other People's Animals

Socialization with other people's animals is best started by:

1. Taking both animals out for a walk on neutral territory.
2. Exchanging puppies part way through the walk.
3. Returning to one household and allowing the now acquainted and relaxed puppies to play for a while. It is best if they play by themselves at this point, without interference from humans.

Leaving Puppy with Others

Leaving a puppy with a friend for a few hours when he is young is an excellent way to help him adjust to times when he must be left at the veterinarian's, in a kennel or alone at home.

1. Take a walk with a friend (preferably the one you will leave the puppy with when you have to go somewhere and cannot take him).
2. When you get back to your friend's house, let your friend feed the puppy while you leave.
3. Stay away for about fifteen minutes. Come back. At first do not greet your puppy—just your friend. When you greet the puppy, do it very casually. If you excite him, he will anticipate (not expect) your return whenever you leave and can become very nervous waiting for you.

"KPT"—KINDERGARTEN PUPPY TRAINING

Now that you know the basic guidelines for starting your puppy on the right track around the house and with your friends and neighbors, it is time to go out and meet the general public. Socialization at this level is extremely important because the puppy must be able to get along in our intimate world. It is important that he learn to relate positively, without fear or aggression, to people and other animals. Although this book gives you the guidelines for

KTP teaches boy and puppy to respect each other.

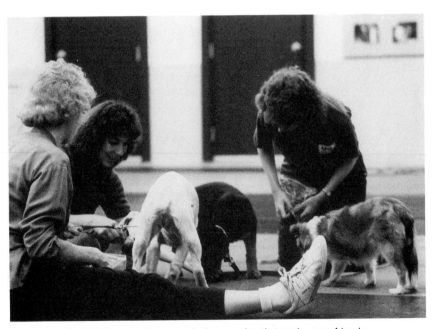

In KPT training, it's not only the puppies that make new friends.

proper upbringing, it cannot duplicate the benefits of activity with other humans and animals. One of the best methods to socialize the puppy and obtain helpful hints at the same time is to take your puppy to kindergarten puppy training (KPT) classes.

To find out if you have a reputable training center in your area, contact local veterinarians, pet shops or breed clubs. *Get recommendations.* Attend classes (by dropping in) before you get your puppy and find out if they offer KPT. If they do, and if you find the facilities clean and the instructors gentle and positive, get your puppy enrolled.

Our KPT classes are for puppies eight to sixteen weeks of age. While some puppies have only had their first inoculations and there is some danger of puppy-prone viruses being shared, we have never had a problem. *All* puppies, dogs and people who come into the center must have their feet thoroughly sprayed on the bottom with a solution of one part bleach to thirty parts water, and all adult dogs must be current with their shots. We find that the advantages of getting puppies and their owners properly started far outweigh the slight chance of illness.

In socializing your puppy you can compare notes and stories with classmates, and usually it is not only the puppies that end up making new friends!

2

Keeping the Puppy Busy

ALL THE GAMES and skills discussed below are designed to contribute to both the fun and the positive upbringing of your puppy. The energy-using exercises act as building blocks that make advanced training easier and enhance the bond between owner and puppy.

Starting grooming procedures at an early age teaches the puppy acceptance of hands-on treatment over all parts of his body and emphasizes relaxed "stays." Grooming also assures the owner of dominance as nails are cut and teeth are cleaned, as the puppy learns to be quiet and tolerate these "housecleaning" techniques.

HIDE AND SEEK

Hide and seek is fun for owners and puppies alike and helps teach your puppy how to come.

1. Put your puppy on a sit-stay or have someone else hold his leash.
2. Hide behind a nearby tree or, if inside, a piece of furniture.
3. Wait five seconds, then call him excitedly.
4. When he "finds" you, praise him with lots of love and a tidbit or ball.
5. Make each hiding place a little harder and a little farther away. Sometimes

Tunnels are easily made or found, and puppies love to run through them or hide in them.

How high it is depends on the climber's viewpoint!

return to your puppy and end the game at that point so he will not think he always has to leave to get you near him.

FIND YOURS

Find Yours teaches early discrimination by smell.

1. Tie your puppy to a chair or have someone hold his leash.
2. Let him watch you put several objects on the floor: a can, bottle, box, telephone. Use a glove or just barely touch these articles when placing them on the floor (you can use this opportunity to clean your phone!).
3. Go back to your puppy, take his favorite toy and hold it in your hands for several seconds, and let him watch as you throw it in with the other objects.
4. Release him and tell him "Fetch!"
5. When he does, praise him lavishly.
6. As he gets good at selecting his toy, use one of your well-scented gloves or socks and put it with similar objects that are unscented. Pretty soon scent discrimination will be an understood part of his life from your viewpoint, not just from his viewpoint.

PUPPY AGILITY

Puppy agility is like a playground for the canine species. Equipment should be made or found with safety in mind, relative to the size of your puppy. *Your* agility with hammers and nails may determine whether you build a castle or find a big piano box. The puppy will not care! The samples shown may be changed or modified, but will give you ideas. Remember, keep your puppy's safety in mind and teach him slowly.

High Jump

At first, try just walking over the jump with the puppy at your side. If that works—fine; if not, put your puppy on one side of the jump and get on the other side. Use a piece of food to coax him over. If you have a leash on the puppy be sure to keep it loose when he jumps. You *never* pull a puppy (or a dog) over a jump.

Bar Jump

Same as above, except start with the bar on the ground. Slowly raise it after each successful jump.

A-Frame

Put two leashes on the puppy. Get on one side of him and have a friend on the other. Use a piece of food and slowly coax him up and down the A-frame. Most puppies want to go over too fast, so be careful. A person on each side helps ensure that he goes up the middle.

Open Tunnel

Use one barrel or tunnel at first, then add two or three more as the puppy learns to move through them. Have a friend pick your puppy up and gently put him in the tunnel while you reach through the other end and coax him to you with a bit of bait or his ball. He will quickly learn to run through it on his own.

Closed Tunnel

Begin as you did with the *open tunnel,* but hold a sheet up at the end of the tunnel the first couple of times the puppy is sent through. As he reaches you the third or fourth time, let the sheet down. Each time, let the sheet down sooner until he can run through and push the sheet up by himself. Be sure to make sure he is secure each step of the way. Do not let the sheet get tangled around him.

Platform

"King of the Hill" is as much fun for puppies as it is for people. All you have to do is put a leash on your puppy (and a couple of puppy buddies!), take a treat and lead him up the ramp to the platform. Let him sniff the entire platform and get used to it, then lead him down another side. Repeat from all directions, then take the leash off and toss a toy onto the platform and watch him figure out the easiest way to get it! Several puppies playing this is a lot of fun to watch.

Playhouse

A playhouse can be used for children and puppies alike. The more inventive you are, the more fun both kids and puppies will have. If you are not handy with a hammer and nails, you can purchase plastic playhouses, or go to a piano shop and get a piano box. The easiest way to familiarize the puppy with the playhouse is to let him follow kids through it, so if you do not have any, borrow some from the neighbors. (This is good socialization for your puppy *and* the neighbors, and it ensures that they will watch out for your puppy!) You can also hide various toys in the playhouse when puppy is not looking.

Accuracy comes with maturity, as this Sheltie shows how to snatch her toy from the air.

These are just a few of the objects you can use. Others are small sway bridges, slides, kids' wading pools with a little water, tire jumps, mazes, tether balls hung low and tents. Only your imagination will limit the playground!

SOCCER

Soccer is an excellent game to play to exercise both you and your puppy. It teaches him coordination, concentration and the ability to wait.

1. If you have a big puppy, start with a soccer ball; if not, start with a small rubber ball, bigger than mouth size.
2. Start "herding" the ball with your feet and let the puppy follow you and watch.
3. Kick the ball slightly to the side and in front of you and let the puppy go to it and smell it.
4. Start herding it again with your feet and then kick it to the side again. Excitedly tell your puppy "Push it." If he moves it at all, praise him highly. You may have to stick a little bit of cheese on the ball to get him to move it at first—that's okay. Soon he will get the idea and it will be a challenge for you to keep up with him. Many dogs I know spend hours herding their ball all by themselves.

FRISBEE

Frisbee is another game that teaches coordination and direction. It can be taught as soon as your puppy knows how to fetch.

1. Take a Nerf, Frisbee or ball, or a wadded-up sock (you don't want a hard object to hit soft gums and discourage the puppy from trying), and hold it above the puppy's head, near his mouth.
2. As soon as he opens his mouth, drop the ball into it and praise him for the "good catch."
3. Repeat several times. When he is eager for it, try holding the ball higher.
4. If he catches it, step a foot away and tell him to wait, then toss it right to him, just above his head, as slowly as you can.
5. As he learns to catch, get farther away.
6. When he is very good at it, start throwing it up higher and just beyond him. As he gets better, increase the height and distance, and soon you and he will be playing Frisbee!

PUPPY TRACKING

Puppy tracking is a wonderful way to get you and your puppy out for a walk two or three times a week. Tracking is natural for a dog and easy to teach, at least for short distances.

This Dalmatian puppy is hot on a "tuna fish trail"!

A long line ensures that your puppy will return to you with his prize.

33

1. Find a park or nice open area. The initial site does not need to be very big.
2. Tie your puppy to something and let him watch you "lay a track" by placing tidbits on the ground one foot apart in a straight line for ten feet. Also let him watch you put his favorite toy at the end of the track.
3. Walk back through the same track to the puppy.
4. Take him to the first piece of food, point to it and say "Track." Encourage him to put his head down and keep it down by pointing to the next piece of food. He will quickly start smelling from piece to piece!
5. When he reaches the toy, praise him lavishly and play with the puppy and the toy.
6. Repeat three times.

If you practice two or three times a week on short tracks, he will become pretty reliable pretty quickly. As his nose keeps to the ground, spread the treats a little farther apart each time you "track." When he can go fifty yards in one direction, lay another "leg" at a 45-degree angle to the right or left.

You should also have someone else start laying the tracks so that the puppy will learn to track different people. Do not try to hurry things along by going too far too fast or by making too sharp turns. If you get really interested in tracking, find an instructor who can help you with some formal tracking. Many six-month-old puppies have tracking degrees!

PUPPY FETCHING

Puppy fetching is important and helpful. It both uses energy and teaches the puppy to return to you. Again, this exercise will help as a basis for more advanced training later on.

1. Find a toy your puppy really likes. Sometimes this can be difficult if your puppy is the type that does not like to play (and there are those types—it's up to you to teach them to play). I've found that a little agility work can loosen up a reluctant puppy, and when they are all wound up they are more apt to fetch. Try using a soft sock or small stuffed toy.
2. Put your puppy on a twenty-foot line.
3. Put the toy in front of your puppy and back up, waving the toy gently on the floor as you move back.
4. When the puppy first grasps the toy, tell him "Good boy!" and very gently tug it for just a second to make him hold it (no tug of war). Let go and praise him as he carries it. If he drops it, repeat the process.
5. After a few successes, throw the toy a few feet from the puppy and tell him "Fetch." When he gets it, praise verbally and let him carry it for a few seconds.
6. *Gently* pull him to you (do not make him drop the toy by tugging too hard). When he reaches you, offer him a piece of treat for the toy. When he drops

the toy, give him the treat. Repeat until he understands what you want. You will both greatly benefit from this game!

These are just some of the things you can do to build rapport between you and your puppy and at the same time teach him to respond positively to learning so that his advanced training will be easy!

GROOMING

Grooming should be started the day you bring your puppy home. The first week, acceptance is all you are really looking for.

1. Select an old table or put a carpet piece on a good table.
2. Put the puppy on the table and let him sit, lie down or stand.
3. Stroke him gently for a few seconds, then run a soft brush gently over his sides, back and tummy for two or three minutes.
4. Take your fingers and gently rub his gums.
5. Look into his ears, rub them and *smell* them, then look into his eyes and gently rub your fingers around the brows and under the eyes. If you know what the ears and eyes look like and smell like normally, you will know right away when something is wrong and he needs to see a veterinarian.
6. Take a nail clipper and gently rub it around his foot and under his paw (every paw, every day).

The second week, start a little more directly and groom a little more normally.

1. Begin to line brush or line comb the puppy (see p. 81). This allows you to see the skin.
2. Substitute a soft baby brush for your fingers and gently brush the teeth.
3. Continue to check ears and eyes daily. If the ears get dirty, use a cotton swab, slightly moistened with diluted alcohol, to clean them. If the eyes get abnormally runny, see your veterinarian.
4. Start cutting those sharp little nails (see p. 81) by doing just a few at a time. Keep the puppy distracted by tapping the feet and under the paws after cutting each nail. Gradually increase the number you do at a time until you can do all of them without complaint. If your puppy has dewclaws (little toes above the foot), be sure to cut those, too.

If you are conscientious in grooming, your puppy will grow up thinking it is simply part of life. If you neglect it, you are going to have problems!

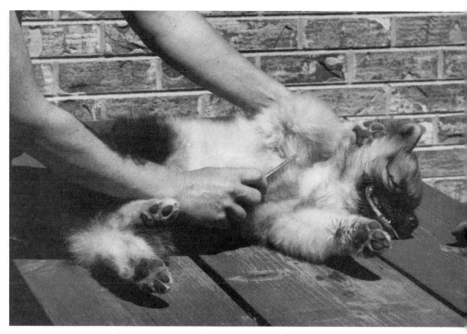

Brushing and combing must be taught at an early age.

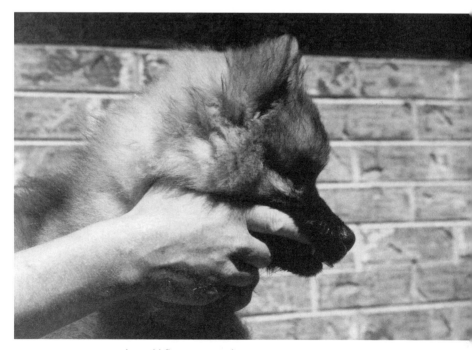

Ice-cold fingers are welcome on sore puppy gums.

Place your hand properly before attempting to sit your puppy. This gives you total control.

Rock your puppy gently back, keeping equal pressure top and bottom to help your puppy keep his balance.

raise your puppy quietly and stroke him for several econds before releasing him.

3

Table Manners for Obedient Puppies

Now THAT YOU HAVE ESTABLISHED a foundation of household rules for your puppy, as he grows you can enlarge his area of learning and responsibilities as you choose. Probably the most important fact for you to understand is the difference between *conditioning* and *training*. If you think of an athlete, think of all the physical and mental conditioning that goes on before that athlete can perform under reflex-type circumstances. It is the same with a puppy. When you teach him to sit, you are conditioning him to respond physically to a verbal or visual command. Until he is able to sit whenever he hears or sees that command, without any physical aid from you, he cannot be "trained" to use that sit. However, once he is conditioned to sit whenever he hears or sees the command, he is ready to "train"—by saying, for example, "Go to Mary and sit." That sentence entails his conditioned responses to *go, to Mary* and *SIT*. If you understand this, you will not expect too much too soon, and because you do not expect too much too soon, the conditioning of your puppy will go smoothly.

It will help if the puppy's first "table manners" are the sit, down, stand and stay, in that order. If you instill these basic commands in the puppy until he is comfortable with them, everything else will fall into place.

These exercises are taught in such a manner that while they instill obedience and respect in your puppy, he will never be cowed by them. If you follow these directions the results will help you accomplish whatever you choose to accomplish with your puppy.

Start with one exercise and practice it six times, twice a day, for a week before proceeding to the next exercise. Decide right from the first if you want an "armchair response" or a "straightback response." Anyone who wants to obtain high scores in obedience-type competitive events must be prepared to be patient enough to achieve a straightback type of conditioning for their puppy. That is, each sit must be straight, squared on both hips, with front toes parallel to your toes. If the dog is to be your household companion or another type of event dog and you do not care how straight he sits, then armchair responses are fine for you. In that case a sit is near your side, back legs down, front legs up. People purchase or receive dogs for different reasons, and the conditioning and training should be designed to give you the results you desire. Armchair or straightback, it's strictly up to you!

Remember to focus your total direction to the puppy on one thing at a time. Try not to do anything with your voice or body that distracts from that focal point. For instance, if you want a puppy to sit straight at your side and you turn your feet toward him to make him sit, how can he do what you want? You must keep your feet straight in the direction you want the puppy to sit in order for him to sit straight! Try to think ahead and plan your movements and voice to enable you to accomplish one single act at a time. This usually guarantees success, and both you and the puppy are happy. Most often, failure and frustration come from talking too much or moving too much. Remember, the puppy is *your* mirror image and will react in kind.

SIT

"Sit" is the first command to be learned. It will become your control over the puppy and his control over himself. The sit is taught using a puppy collar.

1. Put your puppy parallel to you on your left side and kneel beside him.
2. Slip your right hand, palm up, fingers going in the direction from your puppy's ears to tail, underneath his collar.
3. Place your left hand, palm down, across his back, thumb on your side of the puppy.
4. Slide your left hand down your puppy's back, over his tail and around his rump, and just before you reach the hock joint, say "Sit" (quietly) and pull up and back on your puppy's collar with your right hand and push forward with your left hand. In effect, you will sit your puppy right into your hand, where he will be perfectly secure.
5. Quietly praise verbally. Hold your right hand still while you pull your left hand gently from underneath the puppy and use it to stroke him slowly.
6. Count slowly to five, then release him and praise him. Repeat five times.

When downing your puppy, make sure he is secure and relaxed at your side before you start to roll him into you.

As you lift the puppy's front legs up, turn them to the left and pull his body into yours.

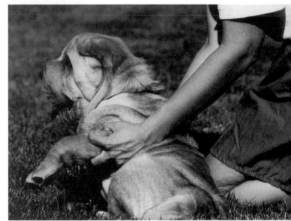

As your puppy rolls to the ground, speak softly to him and keep him down for several seconds before releasing him.

DOWN

After your puppy learns to sit, you may teach him the down. The down is taught using a puppy collar.

1. Kneel with your puppy on your left side. Position your body parallel to his, but this time line up *just behind* his shoulders.
2. Place one hand on each side of your puppy at his shoulders. Your palm should be flat against the shoulder, your fingers pointing to the floor, your thumbs curved around the front of the shoulder blades.
3. Say "Down" (quietly) and gently use the pressure from your left hand against the puppy's shoulder to pull him slightly back and into your body and, at the same time, use your right hand to roll his right shoulder down and away from you. In effect, you are cradling your puppy slightly back into your body and onto the floor. If you have "rolled" him correctly, his front legs will be pointed directly to the left. If you have rolled him incorrectly and tried to pull his front legs forward, he probably will have jumped away or tried to bite you.
4. Leave your left hand where it is and use your right hand and fingers to gently scratch his chest while you quietly, verbally praise him.
5. Count to five (slowly) and then release him. Repeat five times.

STAND

This exercise is very useful when you want the puppy to stand quietly for veterinary care, for petting by children or guests or for examination by a judge. The stand is taught using a puppy collar.

1. Kneel with your puppy on your left, or place him on a table.
2. Have him sit.
3. Slide the fingers of your right hand, pointing up, against the puppy's throat under his chin (your knuckles will rest against the throat). Grasp the collar.
4. Slide your left hand underneath the puppy's tummy (palm up), near his back legs.
5. Say "Stand" (quietly) and gently pull the collar straight forward with your right hand while simultaneously lifting up under the tummy just in front of the back legs with your left hand.
6. Praise verbally, quietly, for ten seconds. If he tries to move, gently restrain him with pressure from your hands on the collar and under his tummy. Release and praise. Repeat five times.

Balancing your puppy at both ends helps him maintain a stand.

If your puppy starts forward, pu[]
your leash up immediately to kee[]
him in a sit position.

STAY

Once your puppy becomes conditioned to being positioned in a sit, down or stand, he needs to learn to remain in that position when you leave his side. Thus far you have controlled his actions with your hands either on his collar or on his collar and on his body. For the stay exercises you will control him from his leash (and balance him, if necessary, with your hand). It is important that you understand that the leash is his *safety net*, not an instrument of torture! In order for him to understand this, you must control him through the leash with a quiet, restraining type of pressure. The leash is not for harsh jerking. It is for controlled restraint. When the puppy realizes he is under your control and cannot make a move, he will look to you for direction. This is what you want. All you have to do is be patient and consistent.

Sit-Stay

The sit-stay is taught using a puppy collar and a six-foot leather leash.

1. Put the puppy at your left side, parallel to your body. You are both standing up.
2. Place your right hand on the leash *immediately* above the collar, between your puppy's ears. Place your left thumb above the puppy's right hip and your left index finger above his left hip (finger and thumb will form a downturned "C").
3. Say "Sit" (quietly) and simultaneously pull up and back with your right hand and gently squeeze your left thumb and index finger into the puppy's hips. These simultaneous actions will cause the puppy to sit.
4. Say "Stay" (quietly). Keep your right hand (palm up) on the leash near the collar until you get the remainder in your left hand. Then let the leash slip through your right hand as you straighten up. If the puppy gets up, slide your right hand back down the leash to his collar and resit him immediately, keeping the pressure from the leash steady. It does not matter if you have to resit him ten times as long as you do it calmly and do not let him make *any* forward progress. He must always be backed up to the point he left and was repositioned in.
5. As he begins to understand what you want, maintain the leash with a slight pressure in your right hand, say "Stay" (quietly) and step directly in front of him. Continue to use your left hand to hold the remainder of the lead (see p. 42). Remember to stand up straight. If the puppy even starts to get up, pull up and back under the leash with your right hand. He is to make no forward progress. Stay in front of him until you can count to five slowly.
6. Step back to the puppy's side and count to five again. Then release and praise him and let him up. Repeat until you have six successful five-second stays. As he learns, increase the time and distance slowly.

Down-Stay

The down-stay is taught using a puppy collar and a six-foot leather leash.

1. Put your puppy at your left side (you are standing).
2. Hold the leash in your right hand, right at the collar. With your left hand against the puppy's left hip, gently pull him onto his right hip (see p. 40).
3. Place your left hand over the puppy's shoulder (fingers to the left, thumb to the right) and say "Down" (quietly), and simultaneously tug down on the leash with your right hand and gently push on the puppy's shoulders with your left hand. He will fold into your left leg.
4. Stroke him for several seconds, then stand up. Tell him "Stay" (quietly) and turn to stand immediately in front of him. Count to five slowly. Return to heel position; count to five and release and praise.
5. If the puppy gets up, redown him exactly where you first put him.
6. Repeat five times. As he learns, slowly increase the time and distance.

Stand-Stay

The stand-stay is taught using a puppy collar and a six-foot leather leash.

1. Put your puppy on your left side in a sit.
2. Put your right hand on the leash, just in front of his neck. Put your left hand underneath his tummy and say "Stand" (quietly); simultaneously pull forward gently on the lead with your right hand and lift up with your left hand.
3. Say "Stay" and stand in front of the puppy. He probably will move toward you. If he does, place your right hand underneath the top of his collar, palm up, fingers pointing toward his tail, and push him gently backward (do not pull up on his collar or he will sit). If it helps as you correct, replace your hand under his tummy as you push him back to help support him in the stand position (see p. 42).
4. Stand in front of him until you can count to five slowly. Return to his side. Count to five again. Release and praise.
5. Repeat five times.
6. As he learns what you want, have other people pet him, but make sure he stands *still* until you return to him and release him.

WITH-ME

"With-me" should mean "Do not pull on the leash" to your puppy. The "with-me" command is taught using a puppy collar and a six-foot leather leash.

As soon as your puppy turns toward you, begin praising him effusively.

1. Follow the directions for leash breaking (Chapter 1).
2. When your puppy approaches four months of age, in addition to teaching him to walk on a loose leash (with-me), you may wish to teach him the "heel" position. This will keep him in a line exactly parallel to you, about two inches from your left leg, with his footwork matching your footwork! For these instructions, see Chapter 8, p. 115).

COME

"Come" is a command every puppy needs to know and respect. Here again, control is essential. When you say "Come," the puppy must have no alternative. Consistency in your conditioning is imperative, for once the puppy realizes he does not have to come, your troubles begin! The come is taught using a puppy collar and a twenty-five-foot line.

1. When you first put your puppy out in the yard on his line, the very first time, allow him to explore until he seems to be getting tired.
2. At that point, kneel and say "Come" and give the line a small, sharp tug. The tug will turn the puppy toward you. He may then:

• Come—If he does this, really love, cuddle and praise him. Pick him up and carry him into the house and give him a tiny tidbit.
• Turn and sit—If he does this, continue to give gentle little tugs, along with lots of verbal encouragement, until he gets to you. Then praise as if he had come on his own.
• Buck and holler at the end of the line—If he does this, sit quietly until he quits (sometimes it takes a while). Then give another "Come" and tug the line again. Repeat—even if it takes fifty waits, fifty "comes," and fifty tugs. When he reaches you, love him and praise him as if he had come on the first call, on his own.
• Sulk, roll over on his back, wrap his feet around the line and say, "No way, José!"—If he does this, stay calm, wait until he freezes in some position, then repeat "come," and give a tug on the line. If he repeats his previous actions, repeat yours. When he finally comes to you, reward him and praise him as if he had come the first time. As you pick your puppy up and carry him into the house, you may tell him anything as long as your voice is happy—you have won—no matter how long it has taken you!

Always remember, the only way you can lose a come battle is to lose your temper. Once you do that the puppy has won because you have given him something to react to. He will know he has upset you and that little piece of information will get stored in his memory bank. So, stay cool!

3. Take the puppy on a twenty-minute walk. Let him go to the end of the line and sniff and snuffle to his heart's content.

4. Four times during that walk—when he is on the end of the line—say "Come" and snap the line toward you and run away from the puppy.
5. When he "catches" up with you, get down to his level and love him, praise him and reward him!
6. Try to take another walk, later on in the day, in a different area and repeat the four calls.

If you use these exercises on the come daily, both at home and on walks, the puppy will grow up knowing that "come" means a problem for him when he remains where he is and does not come, and that safety and praise are his when he does come. Later on, when he is truly free to choose, if you have been consistent, he will choose you. But, if you abuse the welcome or do not enforce the call, the results will not be the same. Therefore, if you find your puppy chewing on your slipper, do not tell him "Come" and correct him for chewing when he arrives. Either go to him and correct him for chewing or call him and reward him for bringing the slipper! A come is always rewarded, even if he has bitten your mother-in-law!

GO

This command is easily taught and can be used later as a helper in conjunction with a second or third command (such as "Go get Dad"). The go is taught using a puppy collar and a six-foot leather leash.

1. Put your puppy on a sit-stay, or have someone hold him, or tie him to an immovable object.
2. Let him watch as you put a treat about two feet in front of him on a box. The box height should be just below the puppy's eye level when the puppy is standing.
3. Go back to the puppy, unsnap his leash, point to the treat and say "Go!"
4. If he goes, let him have the reward and praise him. If not, direct him with your left hand alongside the right side of his head to the treat. After two or three times, he will go!
5. As he learns, increase the box's distance from the puppy until it is about thirty feet from him.

As you finish reading this chapter, consider the next. While the next chapter is intended especially for show prospects, the suggestions continue to teach you about your puppy's nature. The free-lead and hands-on exercises will help your puppy mature into a stable, reliable, happy pet.

Practice makes perfect!

This teenaged Siberian Husky puppy demonstrates free baiting beautifully.

Garlic chicken is a good reason for this Shar Pei puppy to ignore the judge and pay attention to his handler.

4

Table Manners for Conformation Hopefuls

EARLY SHOW TRAINING for conformation hopefuls instills the confidence and that heads-up attitude needed for show dogs to win. These same exercises can benefit good manners for all puppies. Oftentimes a "show puppy" never makes the "show dog" stage, and new owners must prepare themselves for this possibility. Admitting to your friends that your "perfect puppy" did not grow up to be a "perfect dog" is hard the first time it happens. Of course, you could be on the other end, too, as sometimes a dog sold as a pet becomes a champion! Whatever the case may be, early show training is good for all puppies. The exercises in this chapter are designed to teach puppies to react positively to you by keeping their attention on you; you, in turn, reward that attention. The exercises are also excellent for helping submissive or aggressive puppies learn to tolerate strangers.

FREE BAITING

Free baiting is used to keep the puppy's attention on you while the judge takes a look at your dog. It is used when the dog first enters the ring, when you bring the dog back to the judge and when you end your pattern. This exercise is taught using a show lead and bait.

1. Put your puppy's show lead on and let him follow you and drag the leash while you go to the refrigerator and get out his bait.

Compare this Sheltie puppy's free stack position with the next picture's hand stack position. As the puppy grows, free stack training will help proper positioning of the legs without hand stacking.

Here the puppy's legs have been hand stacked (placed properly).

50

2. Put a piece of bait in your hand, hold *both* hands together toward the puppy and show him what you have.
3. Holding the bait near your puppy's nose (in both hands, lead still dragging on the floor), back up and let the puppy follow your hands.
4. Stop and immediately give the puppy a piece of the bait (before the puppy can jump up).
5. After he eats it, back up again and repeat this procedure five times.
6. If he jumps up, stand straight up and say "No" (quietly). Wait until he has all four feet on the floor and he is looking up at you (it may take a minute or two). Only then give him another bite of the bait. In other words, reward for four feet on the floor, ears and eyes attentive to you; withhold reward for any other behavior.

FREE STACKING: WITH DISTRACTIONS

This exercise is taught using a show leash, bait and a friend.

1. Get a friend to play "judge" and have him simply stand still.
2. Take your puppy about ten feet from your friend. Put your leash and bait in both hands and back up toward the "judge" (the leash will be very loose).
3. Back up until you would be shoulder to shoulder with the judge if you were standing straight up. Stop and immediately give your puppy a tidbit.
4. If your puppy wants to smell the judge, let him. Then, using the bait, lead him back a few feet and reapproach. Reward when the puppy gives you his attention.
5. Repeat five more times.
6. As the puppy learns to ignore the judge, have the judge slowly walk around him while you keep his attention on you with the bait.

BAITING TO THE JUDGE

Teaching the puppy to bait to the judge does two things: It helps alleviate fear of strangers and teaches the puppy to look straight into the judge's eyes—which is good showmanship!

1. *After* the puppy has learned to bait to you (you always want to be able to exercise that control), give your judge a piece of your bait.
2. Take your puppy ten feet away and lead him toward the judge, this time with your leash in your left hand and your bait in your right hand. Both of you will be facing the judge as you approach.
3. When you reach the judge, have him bend down and put his hand where your hand is. Leave his hand there and slowly withdraw yours.
4. Let your judge talk to your puppy and feed him bits of the treat.

5. Have the judge stand up and you offer bait to your puppy and reclaim his attention.
6. Repeat five times.

FREE STACKING: REPOSITIONING

You always want your puppy to come in and "stack squarely." This means you want the dog's weight distributed evenly over both front and rear legs (except for German Shepherd Dogs). This allows him to have a body line that is straight toward you from his nose to his toes. In order to achieve that form you need to practice getting your puppy to move slightly backward or forward, or slightly to one side or the other. This exercise is taught using a show leash and bait.

1. Put the bait in both hands and face your puppy, letting the leash drag on the ground.
2. Back up and let the puppy come toward you. Stop.
3. If the puppy stops squarely, give him a treat. If not, take the bait and very slowly put it just above his head. This will move the out-of-place foot back. If you go too quickly, you will move more than the offending foot or you will move the offending foot too far.
4. If the puppy tries to sit when you put the food above his head, lower it under his nose to his chest. He will duck his head and back up.
5. If the puppy jumps up, stand up and put your foot toward him and say "No" (quietly).
6. Practice until you can very subtly move each foot with the bait. Gradually stand up straight as you practice.

HAND STACKING

This is a wonderful exercise for all puppies—those of mixed heritage as well as purebreds—as it teaches the puppy to allow you full control over his body.

1. The head must *always* be the focal point of control. At first use food in your right hand to distract the puppy (hold it just above his natural nose level).
2. Use your left hand to position each leg in a four-square stack (except for German Shepherd Dogs—these dogs are stacked with the right rear leg underneath the right side of the dog's belly and the left rear leg extended behind the left side of the dog). In most cases, a square stack is achieved when the front legs are centered underneath the shoulder blades (elbow lined up under withers) and the rear legs are extended to a point where the "hock" is perpendicular to the floor.

Keeping control of the head allows proper placement of all legs.

This Doberman puppy learns to stand quietly as her owner strokes her under her tail.

Hold still! she says
    Did she ever try?
Hold still! she says
    I don't know why!

Hold still! she says
    It's just my luck
Hold still! she says
    My head's held up!

Hold still! she says
    I can't get free

Hold still! she says
    She's grabbed my knee!

Hold still! she says
    There goes my hock—
Hold still! she says
    When will she stop?

Good pup, she says
    What did she say?
I love you pup.
    I guess I'll stay.

3. Try to move the front legs at the elbow, not at the lower leg or foot. Try to move the rear legs at the hock from the back side or just above the hock from the inside.
4. Start with one leg and just handle it until the puppy is comfortable. Work for ten to fifteen seconds at a time, then praise and release.
5. As the puppy learns to accept the handling, put a piece of his treat on the floor in front of him and slip your right hand, palm up, fingers pointed from ears to tail, under the top of the collar and grasp the collar. Let him watch the bait as you hold his head up with the collar and position his left front leg first. Switch hands and position his right front leg. Switch hands again and position both rear legs (left, then right). Stroke his back for ten seconds, then pick up the bait and give it to him. Praise and release him.

CONDITIONING: THE JUDGE'S APPROACH

This exercise is taught using a show leash and bait.

1. Hand stack your puppy or stand directly in front of him.
2. Feed him as the judge approaches. When the judge stops, hold the bait up for a few seconds, and allow the puppy to look at the judge. When he looks back at you, reward him with praise and bait.

CONDITIONING: THE JUDGE'S EXAMINATION

This exercise is taught using a show leash and bait.

1. Free stack the puppy. Repeat Steps 1 and 2 above as far as moving in front and baiting.
2. As the judge reaches for the puppy, feed the puppy and continue to feed him while the judge gently pets him all over.
3. Let the leash drag on the ground so that the puppy will not use it as an aid. Do not allow the puppy to turn and lean toward or on you. He must stand directly in front of you. It is up to you to instill that kind of confidence in the puppy. Repeat the procedure until the puppy shows no fear of the judge's examination.

CONDITIONING: THE MOUTH EXAMINATION

This exercise is taught using a show leash.

When the puppy totally accepts the rest of his body being examined and when you can examine his mouth without his moving, have your judge examine it. This is often hard for a puppy, so be firm, but patient and gentle. While

The "I," or down and back.

The judge wants the dog directly in front of him, on a loose leash, both going and coming.

cutting teeth, puppies often have sore gums and their tolerance level for someone fooling around with their mouth is not too high. If you have followed your grooming lessons you will find the going much easier on this exercise.

PATTERNS

There are four basic patterns that cover most judging: the "I," Circle, Triangle, and "L" patterns. In all these patterns the objectives are the same: Keep your puppy balanced and in the judge's eye at all times.

Your turns are manipulated so that the dog always remains the center of attention. When you teach your puppy the patterns, you want his head to be up at all times. The turns are made in such a manner that the puppy keeps upright.

To teach the puppy these proper techniques it is important to go slowly and not hurry. Many mistakes are made by getting youngsters to trot too fast, too soon. You want to accomplish all the patterns at a walk, then jog with head up and four feet under before trying to accomplish the same thing at a well-paced trot.

DOWN AND BACK TOGETHER

This pattern is used when a judge wants to compare the front and rear movement of two dogs. Your sole responsibility to the other exhibitor is to start out at each end together. Otherwise, move your puppy at his best pace. For those not interested in showing, this is still an excellent way to get your puppy to pay attention to you while in the presence of another puppy.

1. Depending on your position in the ring, you will start out with your dog on the right or left of your body.
2. When you get to the other end of the ring, turn your puppy in toward you. Do not let him turn toward the other puppy, as you will loose a second or two of control. Face the judge.
3. Wait until your fellow exhibitor has turned his puppy and then start back. When you reach the judge, free bait your puppy by going to his front.

TABLE WORK FOR TOYS AND SMALL DOGS

Many breeds are examined while standing on a grooming table, and it is essential for them to feel totally at ease while on the table. (This also helps for those trips to the veterinarian!)

1. Use a table with a rubber top.
2. When you first put your puppy on the table, put bits of food all around the

To compare front and rear movement, the judge will ask to see your dog alongside another dog.

On this type of "I" pattern, your dog will have to change sides.

Table work is good for all puppies as it gets them ready for easier grooming or visits to the veterinarian.

A properly conditioned show puppy allows you a properly trained adult dog.

table and let him walk around, gobbling up the food. Do this for two or three days without attempting any stacking.

3. When he seems comfortable on the table and eager to get up there, put him up with just a few tidbits on the table. After he eats them, pick him up and reset him and begin to follow the same rules established for hand stacking earlier in this chapter. From this point on there is little difference. Be sure to go slowly and keep his attitude totally positive. When the judge looks around at a tabled dog, it is an eye-level impression and you want it to be good!

In review, here are a few beginner suggestions to help make it easier for you to handle your puppy.

1. Go slowly. Be firm, patient and gentle.
2. Outlast puppy tantrums.
3. Gait your puppy slowly and under control as he grows. Teach him what "straight" means.
4. When you make any turn that will transfer your puppy from one side to the other, transfer your leash from one hand to the other *before* you try the turn; then, turn toward the hand you have transferred your leash to. This will make you turn in *toward* the puppy.
5. Make sure the puppy always turns back toward you. If he moves this way you will always have his attention.

Most puppies learn to shake hands in a matter of minutes.

5

Teaching
Puppy Tricks

PUPPY TRICKS are used not only to entertain yourself and your friends, but also to help the puppy grow in confidence and use his intelligence in a way that makes teaching and learning fun for both of you. The good vibrations that come from teaching tricks helps submissive puppies grow more bold. The lessons teach aggressive puppies tolerance. Teaching a submissive puppy to speak instills great bravado. Teaching an aggressive puppy to roll over, on the other hand, helps the puppy neutralize his fears and conditions acceptance. All the tricks herein either help instill basic obedience, help modify unacceptable behavior or help the puppy use his mind in a way that will help condition him for more demanding adventures later on in life.

TRICKS FROM THE SIT

Shake Hands: One

1. Place your puppy in a sit and kneel in front of him.
2. Take a piece of bait and *slowly* put the bait close to his nose and lead his nose up to your right and back toward his left side. This puts the weight from his body on his left hip.
3. When he leans up toward the bait, his right paw will come off the ground. Just before that happens say "Shake."

4. When he begins to associate the word with his actions you can just reach for his paw and say "Shake," and he will!

Shake Hands: Two

If you have a puppy that really likes to use his paws, try this teaching for shake:

1. Put a piece of bait in your right hand. Show it to the puppy but do not let him have it.
2. Close your hand around the bait and put your closed hand in front of the puppy. Say "Shake."
3. He will smell your hand and "paw" it to get the bait out. When he does, give it to him!

Wave

The wave is an extension of the shake and can be taught as soon as your puppy really understands the shake. Just offer your hand, but instead of saying "Shake" say, "Wave." When he puts out his paw, take your hand away and repeat "Wave." Let his paw come out again, then praise and reward.

Speak

1. Get your puppy excited by tossing around his favorite toy. After a few tosses and fetches, play with the ball in your hands and tell the puppy "Speak." Eventually frustration will cause him to bark. Reward him immediately by throwing the ball. If he does not really turn on with a ball, wait until dinnertime and when he is hungry toss him a little morsel. Then ask, "Do you want it? Speak, speak." Be patient; eventually he will get the idea.
2. If you really have the silent type, try knocking loudly at the door or ringing the doorbell (all things you really do not want him barking at, but if it works . . .). Sometimes something totally unexpected will bring on a bark—if it does, take advantage of it and praise him furiously.

Ride It

"Ride It" can be a lot of fun for you and the puppy, but you need to use caution so that the puppy does not get hurt.

1. Select a ridable item (wagon, skateboard, sled or whatever).
2. Place the puppy in a sit, on top of the object, while you are sitting on the ground with him.
3. Move the object slowly back and forth. Stop it and give the puppy a treat.
4. As he becomes quiet and unafraid of the movement, stand up, and with the

"High-five" is an extension of shaking hands.

"Roll Over" is a good exercise for aggressive puppies, as it teaches them security.

Let your puppy watch while you put a treat into a box.

After you help him get it out a couple of times, let him have a try at it on his own.

Remember, once your puppy has learned to "Open it" no box or its contents will be safe!

puppy sitting in the "wagon" pull it slowly forward. Soon your puppy will become an accomplished rider.

5. This is a lot of fun if you have another dog that knows "Pull It." Then one can pull the other and they can have fun all by themselves.

TRICKS FROM THE DOWN

For the following tricks, the puppy must be able to perform the down.

Play Dead

1. Put the puppy in a down.
2. Kneel in front of him and, if he is not on one hip, gently push him onto one hip.
3. If he is on the right hip, use your right hand to gently push his head and neck toward the floor while your left hand simultaneously leads his nose in the same direction.
4. When his head and neck are on the floor, hold some bait just in front of his nose and restrain him gently, saying, "Dead dog, dead dog."
5. *As soon as* he is still, reward him with a treat and let him up.
6. As he learns, make him "dead" for longer periods of time.

Crawl

1. Put the puppy in a down.
2. Kneel in front of him.
3. Place bait in your right hand and put it in front of the puppy's nose, on the floor.
4. Place your left hand, palm down, just over the puppy's head and shoulders.
5. Back up and say "Crawl." Keep the puppy's head next to the ground with bait and help restrain him from coming off the ground by pressure from your left hand.
6. Work *slowly* or he will jump up. As he learns, get farther away, but until he really understands, he will need you close to him with the bait close to the floor.

Roll Over

For this exercise, the puppy must know how to play dead.

1. When your puppy has "died," take a piece of bait in your fingers and put your hand between his front legs (from his tummy) until your fingers are at his nose. He will tuck his chin toward his chest to get the bait.
2. When he does, pull the bait slowly from his chest in a circular motion that

Puppies One, Puppies All

Puppies one, puppies all,
    Some are short, some are tall.

Puppies black, puppies white,
    Some are heavy, some are light.

Puppies snuggle, puppies piddle,
    Some are big, some are liddle.

Puppies fetch, puppies hide,
    Some want out, some stay inside.

Puppies dig, puppies chew,
    Some smell sweet, some smell—phew!

Puppies jump, puppies tumble,
    Some trot clean, some just stumble.

Puppies lick, puppies wag,
    Some run ahead, some just lag.

Puppies sleep, puppies wake,
    Some like dog food, some like cake.

Puppies sniff, puppies stare,
    Some are coated, some are bare.

Puppies bark, puppies whine,
    Some are yours, some are mine.

Puppies love, puppies give,
    Everyday puppies, wherever they live!

will turn him over, toward the side opposite the one he is now lying on. Simultaneously say "Roll over!"

3. You may have to help him a little once he gets on his back, as many puppies decide at that point to turn back the way they came (especially aggressive puppies).
4. As he learns to roll over, you can move farther away until your circular hand motion and the command will cause him to do the trick by himself. Be sure to reward him each time he gets all the way over.

TRICKS FROM THE STAND

Nerf Catches

This trick is great fun for both of you!

1. Get a soft Nerf toy and teach the puppy to fetch it.
2. Once he enjoys fetching it, hold it above his head and say "Catch."
3. When he jumps up and opens his mouth, drop the Nerf and let him "catch" it. You may have to start almost at nose level. Make sure his head is raised completely.
4. As he learns, begin to toss it instead of dropping it and pretty soon you will have him playing Nerf Frisbee!

Open It

This leads to lots of fun tricks in the future (some you will think up and some he will think up!). It will teach him to use both his mouth and his paws and will teach you what he can accomplish with those tools constructively—as well as destructively!

1. Get a box approximately twelve inches by twelve inches by ten inches and put it on the floor (let your puppy watch).
2. Put a treat in it and allow him to get the treat out and eat it. Repeat two or three times.
3. Put a lid on the box at an angle so that it is not closed but just resting on top of the box so that the puppy can still see inside.
4. Put a treat in and let the puppy push the lid aside to get the treat. Repeat several times, moving the lid a little each time, until eventually the lid fully covers the box but is not down tight.
5. When you see him start using his nose or paws to push the lid aside, push the lid down just a fraction of an inch. Continue putting treats inside.
6. As he learns, push the lid down tight. (Then put all boxes you do not want him in where he cannot get to them!) If he learns this well and has fun at it, see Chapter 10 and teach him a more advanced trick: Go hide!

Following conditions bonding and leadership.

All dogs should be taught to walk near you on a loose leash without pulling.

6

Introducing an Adult Dog to Your Household

BRINGING home an adult dog is quite different from bringing home a puppy. His adaptation to your way of living will largely depend on his previous treatment and environment.

In most cases firm rules and abundant kindness will win him over. Time is in your favor, so use it! If you expect the dog to adapt in a few days or weeks, change your thinking: It will be six months to a year before he is really yours. All dogs should be kept under physical control, that is, fenced or leashed, for that period of time. Unlimited walks will help the adaptation process, especially if you walk in different directions, covering different territories. This helps your bonding with the dog, and the walk back, always leading to his new home, will help him become used to his new "den."

As with the puppy, the following guidelines should help you in conditioning the new adult dog to become socially acceptable.

GUIDELINES

Housebreaking

1. Keep the dog tied to you for the first two weeks when he is in the house. Let him loose in your yard to potty or take him on lead to where you want him to potty. Always tell him "Potty" and praise when he does so.

2. Keep a close eye on him during the third week and let him off the leash in the house for short periods of time. Let him out frequently.
3. If you have a Toy breed or Toy mix, or a dog raised and previously kept in a kennel, your time frames should be a month each for Steps 1 and 2.
4. Do not leave the dog alone to roam the house. If you leave, put him in a secured yard or pen, or in a crate in the house.
5. As time goes on, you will be able to tell if he has good intentions of seeking the outdoors to relieve himself. Depending on the dog and his former circumstances, he may be reliable from the first day you bring him home; alternatively, it may take three or four months.

Sleeping Quarters

1. Select the place you wish the dog to sleep.
2. If it is in the house, let him out shortly before you go to bed or take him for a walk.
3. Tie him on a fairly short lead to keep him where you want him to sleep. Give him his own rug and a small bowl of water, or provide a bed or crate for him.
4. If you want him to sleep outside, provide him with a doghouse or a dry, warm corner underneath a porch or a wind-sheltered corner with some type of protected covering. Make sure your yard is secure.

Crate or Pen Training

If the adult dog was raised using a crate or pen, he should easily adapt to one in your home. If he is not accustomed to it, the best way to adapt him to this confinement is to make the crate his kitchen as well as his bedroom!

1. Make sure the crate is of ample size. The dog must be able to stand up easily, turn around and stretch out.
2. On the first night he comes home, put his food just inside the crate and leave the door wide open.
3. Each night thereafter, move the food closer to the rear of the crate until the dog is comfortable going in and out.
4. One night put a dog cookie in just before his dinnertime. Let him go in and close the door. Wait two or three minutes, then feed him—again closing the door. When he finishes, let him out. Repeat for five days.
5. By this time he should feel pretty friendly toward the crate and may be entering it during the day by himself. It helps if you leave tidbits of food or toys in at varying times. Start leaving the crate door closed after his dinner for several minutes, then for one-half hour or so.
6. Never abuse the time you wish your dog to spend in the crate, but do not feel you are being mean if you use it correctly. Dogs sleep a great deal of the time anyway and will naturally seek a cave. This crate will serve as that

cave. As long as the dog gets adequate exercise (that does not mean lying around the backyard!) during the hours he is out, he can be crated for several hours at a time if necessary.

Leash Breaking

One would hope that the adult dog has been properly leash broken, but if not:

1. Select the proper collar (get help from a knowledgeable pet shop owner or trainer) and buy a good six-foot leather leash that is comfortable in your hands.
2. If the dog pulls when you let him out on the leash for a walk, snap him back sharply with both hands in the handle of the leash. When he stops, praise him lavishly—both verbally and physically. By snapping him back from the end of the six-foot leash you will not be aggressively confronting him but instead giving him the chance to come to you for praise.
3. Each time the dog pulls, correct him sharply—no exceptions. Be sure your praise is as warm as your correction is hard so the choice to pull or not to pull becomes easy for him to make.
4. If you have a good obedience school in your area, consider enrolling in a beginner class. The instructors should be able to assist you with problems that come up. They can often "read" the dog in a minute or two, and even if they do not know why the dog is misbehaving in a certain way, they can often help you correct the problem.

Tying Your Dog to a Chain

This should be done only as a last resort for most dogs. If you get a very placid, easygoing dog, tying him up may be all right. But for most dogs it creates frustration, and frustration can result in aggressive behavior. If you do not have a yard for the dog, then build a chain-link pen and put a doghouse in the pen. Take him for plenty of long walks and encourage him to do things that will wear off the pent-up energy. Read Chapter 7 for some energy-releasing things to do with your dog.

Don't Chew That!

I frequently get calls from owners of "transplanted" dogs asking how to keep the dog from chewing. Oftentimes this is the only problem they are experiencing. It is often the reason the dog ended up in the humane society to begin with, so you can assume that it is a longstanding problem. Your job is to control his actions and create a diversion for his energy.

1. Confine him or tie him to you so he cannot put anything in his mouth that you do not give to him.

2. Get a field dummy (a solid canvas cylinder used for training hunting dogs), put him on a lead and take a walk.
3. Pet him a lot on the walk and handle the dummy a lot.
4. About halfway through the walk, toss the dummy in front of you and let him go pick it up. Tell him he is wonderful and let him carry the dummy as long as he wants.
5. When you get home, take the dummy from him and put it up until your next walk. If he does not like the idea of giving it up, offer him a piece of food in one hand and when he drops the dummy to get the food, pick the dummy up and reward him for the drop with the food.
6. Slowly accustom him to fetching different things for you, such as the newspaper, your slippers or kids' clothes that did not make it to the hamper. This will also assist your bonding. It will not only make him helpful to you, but he will feel good about himself. This combination will help alleviate the frustration caused by chewing. It will take time, so be patient. Your attention to him will solve much of the problem.

Barking

Barking in an adult dog is fairly easy to cure, as he is usually barking from lack of attention (which you are now going to give him). If you follow the puppy rules for barking (see pp. 15–17), that should alleviate most of your problem. If the dog is used to barking when being left outside, for at least the next six months you must not leave him outside when you are gone. If you cannot correct him, you will only reinforce the habit. If he barks when you are at home and he is outside:

1. Half fill a used coffee can with pebbles and tape on the lid.
2. When the dog barks, go outside and quietly say "Quiet." If he quits barking, praise and reward. If he does not, throw the can just behind him and repeat "Quiet." The can will frighten him, and he will stop barking and turn toward you. When he does, praise and reward.
3. At odd intervals, when the dog is quiet in the yard, go out and reward the quiet behavior with praise and a tidbit. Make it very clear after that: either the can of rocks for barking or tidbits for being quiet (but always be sure he is not barking at something that needs barking at).

Biting

Biting is obviously one reason someone would get rid of a dog. Dogs usually bite out of fear, although they may bite if they have been allowed their own way and someone tries to change that way. I have had more than one call from an owner whose own dog would not let him into or out of a certain door, or who would not let them on the couch. Most dogs' biting problems can be alleviated by the average dog owner. Some can be alleviated by a professional trainer. Some problems cannot be resolved in a reasonable manner and eutha-

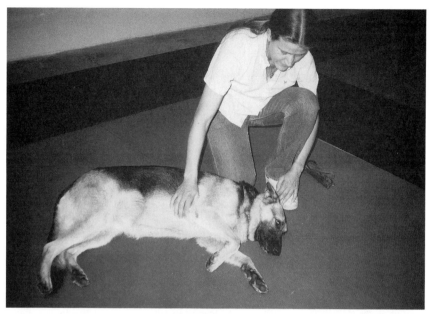

When conditioning a frightened dog to lie down, make sure he is comfortable with you alone before making him lie down with others.

Introduce other people and dogs slowly, as your dog gains confidence in you and himself.

nasia is the best available answer. In determining which of these categories the dog fits into, I use what is called the "love and water test":

1. Give your new dog lots of love and sensible rules to live by.
2. The first time he growls or snaps, go and get a large bucket of ice water. Do exactly what you did to make him growl or snap in the first place.
3. If he growls again, throw the entire bucket of icy water straight into his face and say, in the most degrading voice possible, "Shame on you."
4. Walk away and ignore him for one-half hour and then treat him as if nothing had happened.
5. An hour later refill your bucket and repeat the action that caused him to growl or snap. Either praise him for not growling or snapping or dump another bucket of water over his head. Repeat the entire process one more time.
6. If he does not quit after the third correction, you need professional help. Call your veterinarian or friends and ask for recommendations.

Biting others is almost always caused by fear, and the only way to overcome it is to resocialize the dog. For this you need help. A good trainer knows how to ignore your dog while making friends with you and can transfer the dog to himself within a few minutes. This is a beginning for the dog. If you cannot get to a training center:

1. Try lots of long walks, with lots of friends, on which the dog is not acknowledged.
2. Let your dog follow as many people as possible.
3. Sit down in a public area and calmly eat a sandwich and give your dog tidbits every time he ignores the crowd and pays attention to you.
4. Get your dog in public for several hours each day. If he is actually aggressive and tries to bite when not confronted, put a no-bite muzzle on him. This will allow close public contact without you or the public being in danger.
5. When he is more relaxed with you, make him lie down on his side, with his head down. Keep him there until he falls asleep. Do this first in areas comfortable for your dog with just the two of you. As he learns to trust you, and begins to relax on his side, take him closer to activity and repeat the same exercise. If he gets friendly with one of your friends, have your friend walk him and repeat what you have been doing. One friend will lead to another. The more people that are gentle with him and he accepts, the better chance you have at rehabilitation. You must remember, however, that the dog always has the capacity to revert to a fear reaction, so supervision of this animal will probably need to last his lifetime.

Jumping on People

1. The first rule for everyone connected with a dog that jumps on people is to not touch him unless he absolutely has all four feet secured to the floor.

Broken legs, broken fists
Cut up knees, twisted wrists
Cracked back skull, fractured ribs
Crushed tailbones, crying kids
Plant your feet or watch your rear
Cause that big pup is darn near here!

Submissive behavior disappears when the dog has something to do and can feel good about himself. This Bernese waits patiently for children to fill her wagon.

2. When the dog jumps up, face him and grasp him by the *elbows* and force him to walk backward as quickly as possible until he falls over. Do not let children try this as they will probably grasp the dog's legs and get themselves bitten.
3. If your dog gets clever and quits jumping on the front of people, and thinks it is cute to hit them from behind, set him up. Have a bucket of ice water in your hands and walk away from the dog. When you feel him just about to jump, or when your accomplice says "Now," dump the ice water over your shoulder onto his head.

Submissive Behavior

See Chapter 1, submissive urination and eye contact, and follow those exercises, as well as using this one.

1. Get into a general obedience class. Make sure the instructor is experienced and knows how to deal with this behavior. Corrections must be *positive;* negative ones will reinforce the submissive behavior.
2. Make the dog useful. This helps more than anything because it builds the dog's confidence.
3. Spend a good deal of time repeating the eye contact exercises in various places where the dog shows fear. As he becomes able to concentrate on you in more and more places under more and more circumstances, his confidence will increase.

Eye Contact

Making eye contact with an older dog is harder to do because the dog has practiced avoiding it and has had more time to become either more fearful or more aggressive with regard to the avoidance.

If you have given a home to a dog that you find you really cannot control, you must get professional help or give the dog to someone who can give the dog professional help. Many kindhearted people have generously given of their time to try to help dogs that should, unfortunately, be put to sleep. Many times these well-intentioned folks must be faced with a tragedy, like a badly bitten child, before they can bring themselves to deal with the problem rationally. It is a sad situation, but with the overpopulation of dogs it is bound to occur. If you find yourself in this position, remember that there are *millions* of dogs that need homes, and if you cannot help one, then you can surely help another.

Eye contact is often the way you find out that you cannot deal with a fearful, aggressive dog. If they feel threatened, as they may by direct eye contact, they will lunge directly at you. If this happens, get help. If, when you have eye contact, the dog tries to get away, you have a much better chance of rehabilitation.

1. Have a *big* piece of liver ready.
2. Put the dog on a choke chain and six-foot leash.
3. Stand directly in front of him with the leash in your left hand and the liver in your right hand. Give a correction—a sharp jerk—on the leash straight toward you and say "Watch." The second the dog turns toward you, shove the liver into his face. Do not wait for eye contact.
4. The dog will be astonished. He may back away, grab at the liver or give you eye contact.
5. If he backs away or gives you eye contact, talk to him quietly and offer him the liver again. If he does not want to take it from your hand, toss it on the floor. Repeat the exercise and soon he will listen for "Watch" and know a treat is coming. When that occurs, insist on eye contact before giving the treat—even if just for a second. When you have come this far you can go back to the puppy eye contact exercises and consider yourself successful in obtaining a good start at rehabilitation.
6. If he has snatched the liver, repeat the exercise but this time be ready with both liver and your right foot. If he tries to snatch the liver again, bump his front foot with your toe, but do not say anything. He will look down. Say "Watch" and give another correction, offering the liver again. If he tries to snatch again, repeat the toe-to-toe exercise and say "Watch" again. This time he should look up at you for a second. At that second praise him and let him have the liver. Repeat. Soon he will have forgotten his fear. He will have three things to think about: "Watch" and a correction or reward, eye contact and *toes*. Here again, you have a good start on rehabilitation. Go back to puppy eye contact exercises.

Scratching or Jumping on Doors

This usually is the result of frustration when the dog is left alone. Since the behavior is established, the time needed to correct it may be several weeks.

1. When you are at home, if he jumps up inside on a door, take a large glass of ice water and toss it directly into his face and say "No" (quietly). Turn and walk away. Wait two minutes, then let the dog out. After a few such corrections he should go to the door and whine or sit or just stand there. When he does, praise him and let him out.
2. If he is outside wanting in, use a bucket of ice water when he jumps.
3. If you are not home, crate or pen him. Otherwise his frustration may cause him to totally destroy the door and, given enough time, other objects.

Climbing on Furniture

If you do not want your dog on the furniture, perhaps the two of you can compromise. Get the dog his own bed and see if this does the trick. If it is a Toy or small dog that is using the furniture to look out the window, put the bed next to the window at sill level. This may solve the problem. If not:

1. Leave a long line on the dog and allow him to get on the furniture. Stay ten feet away and the minute he has all four feet up, pop the line and pop him off the furniture. Show him to his bed and praise him there.
2. Until he has learned, crate or pen him whenever you leave him alone.

Fence Jumping

Fence jumping is best solved by using a temporary electric fence. The wire is cheap, and you can rent a charger. Make sure you do not have neighborhood children around, and warn your neighbors that you are going to use it for a few days during certain agreed-upon hours. These fences are not legal in every location. If this is true in your town, this means of correction can't help you.

1. Set the wire eight inches above and six inches inside the entire top of the fence.
2. Create the conditions that you know will send the dog over the fence.
3. Dogs will usually try two, three or four times before they are convinced, so be patient and set him up two or three times for a couple of weeks.
4. After he has hit the wire that many times he will quit trying to jump.
5. There is also a fence available that lies under the ground and reacts to a sensor in the dog's collar. If you want to spend the money to put a circuit around your backyard, this will also work to keep him inside the yard.
6. There are many other physical methods that you can try. Some work on some dogs and some on others, but I have never found any of them totally reliable, and the electric fence works on just about all dogs. Here, again, the more general obedience work you do with your dog and the more you give him to do, the happier he will become and the less he will try to leave the yard.

Escaping

Another common reason why dogs are given up is that some are real natural-born tramps. These dogs are never "lost"; they always return home. But their excursions can be troublesome. They love to raid garbage cans on pick-up day. They delight in calmly trotting by other dogs' yards while the resident barks in fury. They are totally amorous and have been known to leap large fences with a single bound to make more little tramps. They leave calling cards for neighbors' bare feet. They have a variety of other talents that eventually lead them to the pound. Since these dogs are usually the epitome of tail-wagging friendliness, their adoption rate is high. If you are the adopter of such an animal:

1. Neuter him.
2. Put him to work at anything he can possibly do for you.
3. Read Chapter 7 and engage in as many exercises as you both have time for.
4. Make sure you take him on plenty of walks so that if he does get out, you know he can find his way back.
5. Escape-proof your home and build a run with a cement floor and chain-link top. These dogs can get out of unbelievably small openings!

Digging

Digging is as natural as chewing, but the substitute is much harder to use, so preventive maintenance is your best bet. Chewing on trees may follow digging but is easy to stop.

1. Build a run and use pea gravel to a depth of about eight inches.
2. Give him plenty of exercise and constructive play or work to use his energy.
3. Consider the items listed in Chapter 7. The more he has to do, the less frustrated he will become and the less he will try to dig.
4. If he digs only in certain areas you might try laying chicken wire down and staking it on top of those areas. When he digs his paws will run into the wire, and that generally stops most dogs.
5. Chicken wire can also help for those dogs that like to eat small trees or chew on bark. Just wrap the tree to the height the dog can reach.

Socialization with Existing Pets

1. Make initial contact with other dogs *outside* the home. If you can, take your existing dog (or dogs) for a walk and have your spouse or a friend meet you somewhere with your new dog. Take a long walk so the dogs can get used to each other. Switch dogs on your walk.
2. Take all the dogs back to the house. Switch dogs and have a tour of your home, with all dogs still leashed.
3. Let your existing house dogs loose, but keep the new dog tied to you (you will be doing this for some time for housebreaking purposes anyway).
4. If the new dog tries to mark the house anywhere, correct him with a sharp jerk and a stern "No!" If any of the existing dogs try to mark, correct them in the same manner. Explain to all, in no uncertain terms, that marking will not be tolerated.
5. When you feed the dogs be sure to feed the established pets first and stay near the new dog while he eats.
6. Most established pets, if already well socialized, will enjoy a newcomer as long as the newcomer is friendly and is introduced in the manner described above. If you find you have brought in a troublemaker, *you* must remain top dog. If you are not willing to assume that responsibility, take the dog back.

Socialization with Friends

While puppies always generate warm feelings, adult dogs do not. It is especially important that they make a good impression on your friends and neighbors from the start, *especially* if you already have other pets. Set rules for your new dog immediately.

1. No jumping on friends. Keep your dog leashed the entire time friends are at home gatherings for the first few weeks to make sure your dog does not try to jump on them.
2. No barking when the doorbell rings (use a glass of ice water—see "Barking."
3. No running out the door when you open it for guests. Make him sit at your side and ask the guests to ignore him until everyone is in and he has a chance to evaluate the new people. Let him approach them for petting if he is calm; if not, wait until you have established the control you need so as not to make a spectacle of yourself and the dog.
4. When he can accept guests, make sure he does so with all four feet on the ground. It is easy for a dog to try to explore with his paw as well as his nose. If you are firm and consistent from the first guest on, you not only will eliminate obnoxious behavior but will instill acceptable behavior. The end result: Your friends will welcome his addition to your family, not resent it.

Socialization with Other People's Animals

The same logic applies here as with *your* other animals, so use the same type of rules.

1. Take long walks on which you know you will meet friends doing the same with their animals.
2. Contain and restrain your dog from barking at other animals as they approach. If necessary make him sit at your side.
3. Always allow thorough sniffing from both animals, as this is their way of saying hello.
4. If at all possible, invite friends and their animals back to your home and allow the dogs to play by themselves. This solves many problems the everyday pet owner may not think about and he will find the dog much more relaxed and easier to handle. (Aren't you tired and relaxed after having company over? Your immediate problems have been overlaid with good conversation and your energy has been depleted positively. Dogs relax the same way.)

GROOMING

Grooming should be started immediately, both to ensure that you know the dog's body and can spot any potential health problems, and to make the

Line combing allows you to see the skin and check for parasites, cuts, tumors or foreign objects.

Toenails should be cut back to the quick weekly to allow the dog to stand properly on his legs.

Daily brushing helps keep teeth clean and gums healthy.

You've got to be kidding
　　She's smelling my ear!
I thought it was gossip
　　About some poor dear.

But she is just checking
　　To see if I've got
An infection deep down
　　That needs to be fought!

This Scottish Deerhound starts after his prey. . .

. . . and chases it to the ground.

dog realize that he must tolerate grooming—no matter what his previous owner did about his outward appearance.

1. Each day the first week, run a soft brush over his back and down his sides.
2. The second week comb out mats and get the comb down to the skin on the back and sides.
3. The third week start working on the chest, tummy, tail and legs.
4. The fourth week start on nails, teeth and baths.
5. Try to groom at the same time each morning or night, even if only for a few minutes. The dog will come to enjoy it, and the grooming will help the bonding process as well as establish dominance. It will also make the dog look and feel good!
6. Consult your breeder or a good groomer to find out how to groom your particular breed. Make sure he covers coat care, ear care, nail care and mouth care.

Now that your new dog has moved in, let the following chapters give you a variety of ideas about what you and your new friend can do. Some things may appeal to you; others may not. It is all your choice. Your everyday dog, your ever-special dog, will be whatever you make him be!

7

Keeping the Adult Dog Busy

ONLY YOUR TIME and interest will limit the things you can do with your dog. Sports for dogs are more organized now than they have ever been and there are many associations ready and willing to help you get started in whatever type of event you think you and your dog would enjoy. Do not limit yourself to those events that seem specifically designed for a particular breed. While some sports are designed for special breed competition, many fringe sports can include your dog. For instance, agility might seem to be made for German Shepherd Dogs or Border Collies, but the photographs that follow show that even the smallest dogs, if agile, can enjoy the courses and earn titles. There is a wide variety of activities open to you and your dog. The following are fairly widespread available sports, but this list is far from complete.

FRISBEE

Frisbee can be played in every backyard and park and can be started with youngsters (see Chapter 2). Frisbee is wonderful exercise, can use up a lot of energy and keeps your dog in great shape.

A sure catch!

This ten-inch Miniature Pinscher conquers a six-three A-frame. . .

. . . and negotiates a twelve-foot teeter-totter.

A Shetland Sheepdog speeds through an open tunnel.

FLYBALL

Flyball is an excellent team sport. Four dogs are on a team. Each dog, in turn, races over three jumps to a flyball "box." They hit a foot lever with their paws and the lever releases a ball. They catch the ball, then race back over the jumps. The first four-dog team back with the ball wins. The dogs are absolutely wild about this sport. Any dog can participate, as the jumps are set at the jump height of the smallest dog on the team. Rules and sport requirements can be obtained by writing to Mark Jacobson, 10990 Watson Road, Bath, Michigan 48808.

AGILITY

Agility work for dogs is similar to grand prix events for horses. All sorts of jumps and hoops, contact equipment (A-frames, teeter-totters, dog-walks, and so forth) and tunnels are used to test the dog's agility. There are several different associations and each has its own type of equipment, but even on the most demanding equipment most agile dogs are able to compete. The primary goal in agility is to complete the course safely; the secondary goal is to complete it quickly. Most dogs learn agility maneuvers on the smaller equipment in a few days, often well enough to qualify for basic competitions. On the larger equipment much time is spent in teaching the dogs safety, control and direction, and all instructors will caution newcomers to proceed *slowly*. The following people represent three associations you can contact for information:

Kenneth A. Tatsch
P.O. Box 850955
Richardson, TX 78085
(214) 231-9700
(214)783-3800

Mrs. Marilyn Baskin
11656 Coal Creek Heights Drive
Golden, CO 80403
(303) 642-7557

Charles Kramer
401 Bluemont Circle
Manhattan, KS 66502

OBEDIENCE COMPETITION

Obedience is not only nice to have at home but can be a wonderful sport for you and your dog. This competition demonstrates the dog's ability to

This Doberman completes a retrieve over the high jump.

A handler continues to practice hand stacking her Irish Setter even though he is already a group winning champion.

function as a companion and helpmate of man and shows his ability to perform in public places and with other animals.

There are three increasingly difficult levels of obedience competition. The first level, called Novice, demonstrates basic obedience and steadiness. The required exercises include on- and off-leash heeling; a brief examination of the dog by a judge while the handler stands away; a recall where the dog must answer his owner's first call from about thirty feet away; and group sits and downs where the dog must stay in the specified position with six to eleven other dogs for a specified time while all the handlers remain about thirty feet from the dogs. The second level of competition, called Open, includes a recall with a down required about halfway between the dog's original sit-stay position and the handler, who is about thirty feet from the dog; fetching, both on the flat and over a high jump; a broad jump, where the dog must jump a series of boards that are almost flat on the ground; off-leash heeling; and "out-of-sight" sits and down-stays, where the dog remains with six to eleven other dogs for a specified time while the handlers are out of sight. The third level of competition, called Utility, involves scent discrimination, where the dog picks out his handler's articles from articles another person has scented; hand signals, which lead the dog through all the first-level exercises, with no verbal commands allowed; directed retrieve; a moving stand for examination, which requires the dog to stop while the handler keeps moving; and directed jumping, where the dog must leave his handler, travel in a straight line until his handler commands him to sit and then stay in a sit until the handler indicates one of two jumps available—whereupon he must jump that jump and return to the handler.

Each level of competition must be passed under three separate judges before the dog can move on to the next. When all levels have been completed the dog and handler may try to obtain an obedience trial championship. Rules for this sport may be obtained from the American Kennel Club, 51 Madison Avenue, New York, New York 10010; from the United Kennel Club, Inc., 100 E. Kilgore Road, Kalamazoo, Michigan 49001-5598 for purebred dogs; and from AMBOR, c/o New England Obedience News, 70 Medford Street, P.O. Box 105, Chicopee, Massachusetts 01020, for mixed-breed dogs.

CONFORMATION COMPETITION

Conformation competition is designed to evaluate purebred dogs on the basis of how closely they conform to their breed's standard of perfection. Regular classes include Puppy (under one year); Novice (usually immature youngsters, but over a year); Bred by Exhibitor; American-Bred; Open (usually mature adults—often the most competitive class); and Best of Breed competition, which includes the Winners Dog and Winners Bitch and those dogs that have already attained their championships. The sexes are divided in the classes and championship points given depending on the number of entries in the breed and in the sex. If the dog completes a championship it usually makes him more valuable to the owner in a breeding program.

These shows give breeders a chance to compete and to exchange views and see dogs they might want to consider when trying to better their own line. If you have never been to a dog show—go! It is amazing to see more than 130 breeds, ranging in size from a three-pound Pomeranian to a 180-pound Saint Bernard and in every type of coat from the thick-coated Chow Chow to the corded Komondor to the almost coatless Chinese Crested! If you stay long enough, you will see the Group competitions, where the best dog in each breed competes against other dogs from his own Group (that is, all terriers, all sporting dogs, all herding dogs). There are seven groups: Sporting, Hound, Working, Terrier, Toy, Non-Sporting, and Herding; the winners of each group compete for Best in Show. A copy of the rules governing dog shows can be obtained from the American Kennel Club (address listed above in "Obedience Competition").

TRACKING

Tracking is a great way to get your exercise and wear the dog out. It is just what it says: The dog follows a track laid down by another person. An article of the owner's is placed at the end of the track, and the dog must find that article by following the track. It is often said that a tracking test builds real character, as the terrain is often difficult and the weather completely undependable; since the owner cannot assist the dog in any way, everything seems to be left to God and the dog! Training is more time-consuming than difficult, and it requires patience.

Several different tests are available from different associations, with different degrees of difficulty. Basic tests cover short tracks that have only a few turns and a short lag time between laying and running. More difficult tests include more turns, cross tracks, and several items left on the track to be found, with a longer lag time between laying the track and running it. There are several good books on tracking and general information can be obtained from the American Kennel Club (address listed above in "Obedience Competition").

HUNTING

Hunting is as natural as walking to many dogs and by using natural talents they can perform both vigorously and happily and give you physical rewards as well. Anyone who has worked with his dogs in the field, whether hunting birds or small game, will tell you that there is nothing as thrilling as watching his dog work the field, fetch game or take a point and hold it.

Tracking is a great sport that will keep both you and your dog in good physical condition.

A versatile Golden Retriever practices her retrieves. This is a real everyday dog having titles from the bench, in the field, in obedience and in tracking. She also does media work in print and on film.

Celebrating a holiday with fresh game provided by your own hand and delivered to you by your own dog is a luxury in itself.

If hunting is part of your life and you are interested in field training, contact your local breed clubs or the American Kennel Club (address listed above in "Obedience Competition"). There are many types of competitive events available for hunters and information may be obtained from the AKC on field trials and hunting tests for sporting dogs and field trials for hounds, all at varying levels of competition.

SLED RACING

Sled racing can be anything from a friendly competition between two men and their dogs to a competition as strenuous as the thousand-mile Iditarod. Here again, the dog's natural talents are emphasized. While Arctic breeds are most visible, many other breeds (including Poodles and Irish Setters) or mixed breeds can be very competitive. For more information contact your local sled dog clubs or write to the Rocky Mountain Sled Dog Club, Inc., P.O. Box 25, Castle Rock, Colorado 80104, or the ISDRA, P.O. Box 446, Nordman, Idaho 83848.

WEIGHT PULLING

Weight pulling has long been a favorite sport for the Alaskan Malamute and Samoyed breeds, but in the past few years this competition has spread to many other breeds, including—of all things—the desert-dwelling Basenji. Pulling divisions are divided by weight and experience. Dogs are put in harness and must pull a sledge loaded with varying amounts of weight for varying distances in order to earn their points. For further information contact the International Weight Pulling Association, c/o Mark and Pam Johnson, P.O. Box 994, Greeley, Colorado 80631.

HERDING

Herding competition has long been recognized in European countries and has been found in many forms in the United States. Many communities have stock dog fancier clubs or associations. Several breed clubs have initiated herding instinct tests, and the AKC has just initiated a Herding Instinct Test. These beginner levels allow you to assess any possible herding instincts in your dog and allow you to see if that type of competition would be of interest to you. "Real" herding—gathering, driving and penning, as performed by the working stock dogs—is an event that will catch your heart if you are at all interested. To see these intent animals working stock at great distances all on

This little Sheltie shows definite herding instinct and easily passed her first herding instinct test.

their own is truly amazing. Contact your local breed clubs and the AKC for information on beginner-level work.

LURE COURSING

Lure coursing is somewhat akin to Greyhound racing but is held in fields with twisting courses over uneven ground. Lure coursing is designed to test a dog's agility, as well as speed, endurance and prey instinct. The dogs are taught to chase a lure (really a plastic bag!), and their enthusiasm for the chase is an unforgettable sight. For more information contact the American Sighthound Field Association, c/o Sandy Wright, 1235 Pinegrove Road, Kenone, Pennsylvania 17331.

THERAPY DOGS

Therapy dogs are increasing in number by the day. Nursing and convalescent homes, centers for gifted children and even hospitals are opening their doors to visits by therapy dogs. These dogs can be of any age or breed (some organizations request only registered therapy dogs; others welcome any well-behaved and loving pet) and are only expected to be very stable and accept much petting and loving from the residents they are visiting.

These dogs can sometimes elicit responses from the ill or handicapped better than nurses, doctors or even family members. Most dogs instinctively realize when a human is suffering some form of handicap. I will never forget the sight of a large and powerful Schutzhund-trained German Shepherd Dog who was in class one day when about twenty mentally retarded children came to visit. I had asked that all handlers be very careful and keep their dogs at their sides while I ran a demonstration, but when the children entered the room they were led by a large boy who was excitedly waving his arms, obviously in awe of the dogs. When the Shepherd saw the boy he immediately broke from his owner, rushed to the boy and leaped on him. My heart went to my throat, but the feeling of fear was immediately replaced with tears as we realized the Shepherd was smoothering this child with kisses!

Visits with a therapy dog may be just the thing that will bring relief or happiness to an otherwise ill or hard-to-reach person, and your joy at seeing your dog relate to these people is more than worth every minute of your time.

To find therapy groups near you, inquire of your local Kennel Club or organizations dedicated to the needs of nursing-home residents, convalescents and retarded persons.

These are just a few ideas for you to think about. There are many other organizations devoted to preserving the natural instincts of their breeds, such as the Newfoundland Club of America, which sponsors water tests. Many

A registered therapy dog, this Shetland Sheepdog carefully picks up her owner's dropped keys. . .

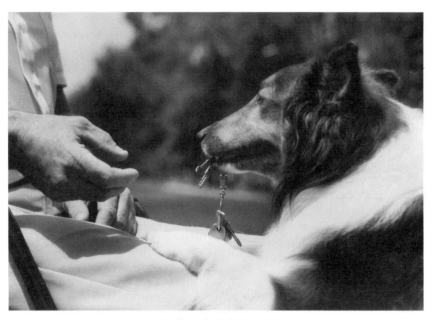

. . . and gently delivers them.

Debbie is owned by the author's husband and besides aiding him at home is an Obedience Trial Champion.

A Newfoundland puppy takes a look at her first body of water. . .

. . . and finds she likes it just fine!

breed or group specialty magazines, such as *Gun Dog,* publish information for fanciers of the upland bird and waterfowl dog. Many major dog food companies, such as Purina, Gaines, Kal-Kan, and Ken-L Ration, sponsor all sorts of hunting, obedience and conformation events. In fact, most fanciers are so willing to share information with you that all you have to do is get in contact with one source and you will be hand-led from party to party until your needs and questions are answered. "Dog people" are some of the very best people to have as friends. Contact them.

When your new dog learns to help you, both of you will feel a sense of accomplishment.

8

Table Manners for Obedient Adult Dogs

CONDITIONING the adult dog who already has his own set of rules requires a good deal of patience. Usually, the initial conditioning seems comparatively easy in that the dog learns quickly, but obtaining consistency from the dog can be difficult. This is because under pressure the dog is likely to revert to his previous behavior for some time—six months to a year—instead of remembering what you have just taught him. The most successful way to modify a dog's behavior is to practice your exercises in a different environment each day. This may not be convenient for you, but it is certainly worth the effort, as establishing control and dominance over your new dog under different conditions will soon convince him that you are definitely in charge.

Conditioning in different places also gives you the opportunity to gain insight into a previously owned dog's former life. If he behaves calmly in quiet surroundings but comes apart when faced with loud noises, he may have been hurt or badly frightened when loud noises were present. If he is calm when you are alone, but uncontrollable when other dogs approach, perhaps he was kept by himself since first sold and had no dogs with which to socialize, or perhaps he lived in a "rough part of town" where he constantly had to fight. In either case, you will have to take the time to properly socialize him if you want a dependable pet.

No matter what you choose to teach your dog, remember that the stay and come are like Siamese twins—you cannot have one without the other. For

If you hold the leash in both hands, and keep your hands together, you will give proper corrections and maintain a loose leash.

If you allow your hands to separate on the leash, the leash becomes tight and the dog will not learn to walk on a loose leash or without a leash and stay near you.

basic control, for bonding, and for a foundation of trust and respect, three exercises you need to teach the adult dog are the sit-stay, the down-stay and the come. The dog should also respect a heel or "with-me" position and not pull on his leash. Once he understands and accepts these basic commands, you can teach him anything else you wish.

Dogs learn best with short training periods (fifteen to twenty minutes), repeated two or three times a day. Your goal should be to improve the dog's response at each training session. The amount of improvement will depend on your efficiency and the dog's willingness. Remember, you not only have to teach an older dog new tricks but probably have to get rid of some of his old ones!

It is extremely important to understand how to elicit a good response from the dog with the least discomfort and most praise. If you were self-employed and had to go back to work for someone else and could no longer arrange your own schedule or come and go as you pleased, you would certainly want your new employer to at least appreciate the talents you were bringing him, recognize those talents and not just stick you in an office and say "Behave and do your work." Try to approach your new dog in the same manner by praising him each time he does *anything* that pleases you, even if he just lies down quietly on his own. He *needs* to know that this is behavior you welcome and he will not realize this unless you tell him.

CONSISTENCY

The most important rule to remember is: Be consistent—teach all exercises in the same basic manner.

1. Verbally tell the dog what you want.
2. Physically position him.
3. Give immediate praise (within one-eighth of a second) after he attains the desired position and reward him with a soft voice and slow strokes.
4. Make sure the dog retains the position you have put him in for a slow count of ten before releasing him.
5. When you release him make sure he breaks the position and turns *to you* for praise.

Remember, he will learn in the exact manner that you teach him. For example, if you sit him squarely on both hips and tell him to stay and he stays but rolls to one hip, if you leave him there, that is the kind of sit you are going to get. If that is okay with you, fine, but if you want him sitting squarely, you must insist that he do so every time you tell him to sit. If you want a straight down position for a competitive event and a separate command for general use, he needs to understand that these are two different things. The command "Down" for the first may be replaced by "Go lie down" for the second. The tone and inflection of your words are what the dog associates with the action, so be consistent.

EQUIPMENT

The type of equipment needed will depend on your ability and the dog's knowledge, size and strength.

Soft buckle collars are good for dogs with gentle, even temperaments. Thin, lightweight, metal choke chains (brass with tight links) that just fit over your dog's head are good for most dogs—those generally well behaved and willing to learn. Nylon or parachute collars that wrap around the dog's neck just below his ears and snap together are useful on willful dogs that have no tendency to obey, as these collars act on the windpipe and are, in effect, self-correcting. Pinch collars are sometimes helpful for large dogs with large, thick necks, or for dogs that have lots of thick fur around their necks, and small owners.

Leashes for conditioning should always be from good leather and they should have as little give as possible. After the dog is trained, show or specialty leads may be used.

Long lines should be from twenty-five to thirty feet in length, made of lightweight nylon cord, with a snap at one end and a handle at the other.

If you have acquired an aggressive dog that is liable to bite either you or others, get him fitted with a no-bite muzzle so that humane conditioning may take place.

LOOSE LEASH CONTROL

Before a dog can begin to learn, he must be properly leash broken. If he is, you can go on to the sit, if not:

1. Start the dog on a long line, letting him lead you down the block.
2. When your dog reaches the end of the line and just before he begins to pull, use both hands in the handle of the long line to give him a sharp jerk back toward you (from thirty feet away it must be sharp or he will not even feel it).
3. Let him continue the walk, but whenever he approaches the end of the line, correct sharply back. You do not want to give him the opportunity to start pulling.
4. As he begins to respect the distance he is allowed on the line, praise him. As the walk begins to tire him out and he slows down, reduce the distance allowed to him on the line until he has only ten feet.
5. While at this distance, change directions every few minutes, just before you say "[His name], this way." As you turn, give a sharp tug on the line.

Keep your body position parallel to the dog and your toes pointed in the same direction as your dog's toes to start the sit.

Proper conditioning affects proper sits.

Always give him a chance to respond *before* you tug the line. If he responds and comes with you give him lots of praise!

6. Repeat this procedure for a few days and then work your way down to a six-foot leash.

Always *always* make sure the leash is loose. The best way to ensure a loose leash is to hold it in both hands, the right hand palm up and the left hand palm down just below and *touching* the right hand. As soon as you feel that your hands are not touching, you can expect a tight leash. Do not let this happen. The correction given from the jerk or tug on the leash should mainly come from the muscles in your right forearm. The left hand and arm are helpers. Remember, I cannot say it too often: Keep your hands together while heeling the dog or even taking him for a walk until he is trained.

SIT

This exercise is taught using a collar and leash.

1. Put your dog on your left side. Place the dog's collar so that the ring attached to the leash is directly above the top of the dog's neck. Put your right hand on the leash immediately above the clasp. Place your left hand on the dog's rump—just above his hip bones. Place your thumb on top of his right hip bone and your index finger on his left hip bone. Keep your body and feet parallel to the dog.
2. Give the command "Sit."
3. Immediately thereafter, pull gently straight up with your right hand and apply pressure in the form of a "C" with both the thumb and finger of your left hand.
4. As soon as the dog sits, stand back up, praise him quietly, verbally, for a slow count of ten. Do not let him move during that count.
5. Release the dog by saying "Okay." Step away from him and encourage him to get up and turn toward you for praise.
6. Repeat five times. Do the exercise at least twice a day until the dog sits on command.

DOWN

This exercise will be taught in two parts, using a collar and leash.

Part One

1. Have the dog sitting at your left side.
2. Kneel beside him, *parallel* to his body, just in back of his shoulder.

s your job to make the down a secure exercise.

As the dog rolls into you, make sure his legs go to the left—do not pull them out in front.

Count to ten slowly and make sure your dog is relaxed before letting him up.

3. Place your left arm over the dog's back and grasp his left elbow with your left hand and his right elbow with your right hand.
4. Apply pressure from your left arm toward his body just after you give the command "Down." Slip his front legs to the left as you cradle his body down and back into your arms.
5. Count to ten slowly. Release and praise.
6. Repeat the lesson five times and continue the lesson for five days.

Part Two

1. Have the dog sitting at your left side. Remain standing.
2. Encourage your dog to relax by stroking from his left cheek to the back of his left shoulder and encourage him to lean against you.
3. Wrap the leash around your right hand once, just below the clasp, and move your left hand above and across his shoulders.
4. Give the command "Down" and simultaneously give a sharp tug with your right hand down and to the right and push on his shoulders with your left hand. He will fall to the ground against you.
5. Praise quietly and count to ten slowly. Release and repeat five times.
6. Repeat the exercise until when you say "Down" and point to the ground with your right hand he will immediately lie down.

STAND

The stand is a simple command to teach, requiring only a few extra minutes each day. You can do it before or after the down or sit, and it helps the dog understand the different positions. You can also teach it independently.

1. Choose a time when the dog is not in a standing position.
2. Stand next to him, with the dog on your left.
3. Say "[His name], stand," and use a small treat in your right hand, held right in front of his nose, to get him up. Use your left hand to casually scratch his tummy as he stands. Remain motionless for a count of ten and let him lick your fingers. Do not bother praising; you want him to remain quiet. After a count of ten just leave.
4. Repeat every once in a while as the occasion arises.

STAY

Primary Stay from the Side

This stay is for all positions and is taught using a collar and leash.

1. Immediately upon the dog's breaking position, say "No" and slip your right hand palm up through the top of the collar with your fingers pointing

Bait the dog forward to a stand with your right hand and steady him with your left hand.

Make sure you back your dog into the position from which he broke.

Have your leash ready to force the dog backward. Do not lead him back into position—he will just keep breaking position.

toward the tail, and place your left hand under his tummy just in front of his back legs.

2. With an equal balance from the pressure of your right hand against the collar and your left hand against the tummy, force him backward to the exact place he has moved from and put him in the exact position he was in.
3. Repeat each time he breaks until he stays for a slow count of at least ten, or until you can see him relax into the given position.
4. Release him and encourage him to come toward you for praise.
5. Repeat five times.

Secondary Stay from the Front

Until now both the positioning from the commands and the corrections from the stay have come with the aid of your hands. Since the hands always represent comfort, even the correction is not a complete deterrent. It is time to enforce the commands without that comfort and give the dog more of a choice.

1. Leave the dog on a stay and go directly in front of him. As you leave put the bulk of the leash in your *left* hand (instead of the normal right hand) and put your right hand, palm up, in front of the left hand on the leash.
2. As you stand in front of the dog do not say anything; you have already given him a stay command.
3. If the dog breaks position, slip your right hand forward and up against the leash and snap the dog backward.
4. Reinstate the desired position and count slowly to ten.
5. Return to his side and count to ten again.
6. Release and praise (encourage him to come to you).
7. Repeat five times.

COME

"Come" is a command we all need to teach our dogs, for obvious reasons. It is best taught on a long line. You should never use the "Come" command unless you can enforce the results until you are sure the dog will both understand and obey the command. Otherwise he will quickly learn he only has to come when you have physical control of him.

1. Put the dog on a twenty-five-foot line. It does not matter where you are, but if you are in the house, watch the furniture!
2. When the dog is at the end of the line and interested in something besides you, say "Come." (Do not shout or he will eventually only come when you

shout.) Give the line a sharp jerk and run away from the dog and keep running until he catches up with you.

3. When he gets to you, love and praise him.
4. Repeat five times.
5. Put him on a sit, stand or down-stay and go to the end of your line. Wait for a count of ten, then say "Come." If he comes, praise; if not, give the line a jerk and then praise when he reaches you.
6. Repeat both types of comes six times, twice a day. Also, use the command off line when you know he wants to come to you. For example, put him in another room and fix his dinner. Call to him and wait until you can almost hear him pounding on the door. Then let him in.

GO

"Go" is a very useful command, especially when used with other commands ("Go fetch" the slippers, and so forth). It is easily taught if you use a companion command that allows some type of reward when you first teach the dog and not one that the dog may resent (such as, "Go get your dinner," versus "Go lie down and leave me alone").

1. Always have a definite point to which you are going to send the dog. When teaching the dog the command, always have a reward (toy or treat) at the go-out point.
2. Start with things you know your dog wants.
3. Hold him by the collar and toss the object a few feet in front of him.
4. After a count of five, release him and just say "Go." When he reaches the object say "Good" and leave it at that.
5. Repeat the exercise at intervals, taking opportunity when it arises, but only when you know the dog wants something. Repeat several times a day if possible for a few weeks.
6. Begin to use the "Go" command with other commands. Make sure you can always enforce the second command, which means you must have previously taught the second command (for example, "Go sit," or "Go fetch"; both the sit and fetch must be reliable).

WITH-ME OR HEEL

The difference between these two commands is that one is associated with going for a walk and the other with a formal position requiring the dog to be "at heel." Going for a walk requires the dog to be within three to four feet of your body. The heel requires the dog to be in a constant position about two feet from your left leg, with the area between his head and shoulder parallel to your left leg; his entire body is headed in the same direction as your body.

112

It is not necessary to have the dog's attention (as shown here) when starting the come.

Use a lightweight long line to ensure fast recalls.

Always reward a come with love!

A heel position...

... is a heel position...

... no matter how you look at it.

With-Me

After you have leash broken the dog, just use the six-foot leash and be sure the dog maintains a position approximately three to four feet from you. Use the snap backs if the dog tries to pull on the leash.

Heel

1. Put your dog on a sit at your left side in heel position. Ribbon up the leash and place it in your right hand, palm up, with your left hand just underneath your right, palm down. The leash should be just loose enough so that the clasp hangs down from the collar and the leash comes up from the clasp to your hands. Both of your hands should be placed at your waist.
2. Say "Heel" and start forward on your left foot (the guide foot for the dog). Take several steps, then stop slowly and tell the dog to sit.
3. If the dog forges in front of you or goes to the side, snap him back to you by popping the leash directly to the heel position from the dog's neck. Praise him as soon as he is back in heel position.
4. If your dog lags behind you, do not try to snap or pull him forward with the leash; instead, use encouragement with your voice and pat the front of your left leg.
5. If the dog tries to cross in front of your body, bring your right leg up sharply toward him. With a little dog bring your right foot across your body and stamp it sharply in front of him.
6. Practice heeling forward until your dog can trot briskly at your side in heel position and sit quickly when you stop. Then try some turns, making sure you do not hurry too much at first on the turn itself or *you* will cause the dog to bump into you or lag. Always praise the dog when he is in heel position. Make the sits between heeling last for a count of at least five so that the dog does not anticipate.

FRONT

The "Front" command is designed to help your dog sit straight in front of you after he has come to you. This is a simple exercise and can be taught with a reward. The exercise will also bring the dog from a heel position to a front position.

1. Tell the dog "Come."
2. When he has come near you, show him a reward by placing cheese or a toy in both hands in the center of your body, just above where his head will be when he is sitting squarely and close in front of you. Say "Front."
3. When he works his way to that position reward him.
4. Repeat until the dog will come to you from any direction and do a proper sit in front.

When the dog is front, he should sit squarely in front of you, about two inches from your toes.

116

5. In teaching, *you* hold still; let the dog do the moving.
6. Repeat five times. Try to do this every day.

FINISH

This exercise moves the dog from in front of you to the heel position.

1. Leave your dog on a sit-stay and walk directly in front of him.
2. Ribbon up the leash in your left hand until it is about eight inches from the dog's nose.
3. Give the command "Heel" and move your left leg and arm back as far as they will go, bringing the dog with you.
4. When the dog gets back as far as your left foot, turn his head into you and bring your left leg back up to your right leg, encouraging the dog to follow.
5. Change the leash from your left to your right hand so that when your left foot gets to your right foot, your right hand is on the leash and your left hand is free to help the dog into a straight sit. Praise him as soon as he gets into heel position.
6. Repeat five times. Do the exercise a little more quickly each time until the dog responds to the command without your moving your left leg back.

FETCH

"Fetch" means get it and bring it to me. If you have a dog that naturally likes to fetch, you can simply put him on a long line and toss out what you want fetched, then after he picks it up, gently and slowly pull him back to you. When he arrives take the object and give him a treat. But there may come a time when the dog does not want to fetch what you have commanded, and then you must teach him from the beginning.

There are various methods of teaching the fetch. I prefer and always use a gentle, consistent method that takes about five or six weeks but ensures that the dog will fetch whatever you want, whenever you want, without fear, and will bring it directly back to you. Since it is difficult to use words alone on this exercise, step-by-step photographs of the exercise are provided.

When you start to teach the fetch, plan to take two to five minutes, twice every day, for the first five or six weeks. Always repeat each step six times in a row—successfully—before you quit. Do not hurry! Time is one thing you learn to use as an ally, not as an enemy.

Week One

1. Place the dog on your left in the sit position. Bring the leash around the back of the dog's neck with your left hand and hold it alongside his left cheek with your fingers pointing forward.

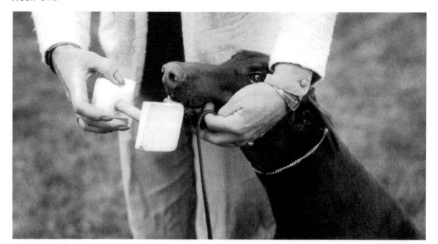

1. With your left hand pull the leash gently forward as you open your dog's mouth.

2. Slip the dumbbell in your dog's mouth and hold your left hand under his jaw to steady the hold.

3. Practice until the dog will hold the dumbbell by himself for about five seconds.

2. Place the object you want fetched in your right hand and show it to your dog. Command "Fetch" and use the fingers from your left hand to gently roll the dog's upper lip against the upper teeth in his mouth. This will cause him to open his mouth.
3. As soon as his mouth opens, slip the object into his mouth with your right hand and slip the fingers of your right hand under his jaw and press up gently for just a second so he will close his mouth on the object.
4. Say "Give" and take the object from your dog's mouth. Give him a treat immediately. Repeat five times (only).
5. If, at any time, he tries to avoid any part of the fetch, correct *only* for the avoidance; that is, get his attention with a snap on the leash and then start at the point he diverted his attention from what you were doing. You want everything to do with the fetch itself to be a positive, rewarded experience, so be sure you correct only for inattention.
6. Do this exercise six times, twice a day, for one week. Your objective by the end of the week is for the dog to hold the object for a count of five without your touching his chin to keep his mouth closed. It is fine for you to physically put the object into his mouth every time. He does not have to be "fetching"—just holding.

Week Two

1. Stand in front of the dog and place the object in his mouth.
2. Put the leash under his chin, but not tight, out to your hand. Tell the dog "Come" and walk back a few steps. When the dog gets to you, say "Give" and take the object.
3. If the dog tries to spit the object out, reach forward and tap him under the chin and say "Hold." When he is holding it firmly, try the come again. Work *slowly*. Do not hurry. Give a treat after each successful fetch. Repeat the exercise six times.
4. Take the entire week—six times, twice a day—to teach the dog to carry the object to you from a few steps away. This is the only objective—do not do any more!

Week Three

1. Have the dog sit at your side. Give him the object (it still does not matter if you are physically placing it in his mouth—he does not have to be "fetching" it).
2. Tell him to "Walk along" or "Heel" and move forward about ten feet.
3. Stop, back up and tell the dog "Come." When he is in front of you say "Sit" and then "Give" and take the object. Then give him a reward.
4. Repeat all week—six times, twice a day. At the end of this week, the dog is now quite comfortable holding, carrying and delivering the object to you.

1. Stand in front of your dog and place the dumbbell in his mouth.

2. Keep the leash slightly tight until your dog takes the dumbbell.

3. As soon as your dog accepts the dumbbell, release the pressure on the leash.

Back up a few steps and coax your dog to you.

2. Stop and tell him "Sit" and take the dumbbell. Really praise him!

Week Four

We are now ready for the dog to begin picking up the object you want on command. He may, in fact, already be taking it from you when you say "Fetch." After all, it has been in and out of his mouth *at least* 252 times if you have done your homework. If he is taking the offered object on command without any physical assistance from you, go on to Weeks Five and Six. If not, take this fourth week and use the following intermediate exercise to get him to open his mouth and fetch by himself.

1. Stand in front of the dog.
2. Put the object against the dog's muzzle, just below his nose.
3. Say "Fetch" and press forward slightly. He should open his mouth. When he does, slip the object in. If he does not open up, reach back and slip your finger under his upper jaw as you did in the first lesson. Praise as soon as he takes the object. Repeat this procedure until he opens his mouth by himself. This is where the extra week comes in. Some dogs just take longer to understand this step. *Do not go on* until the dog will open his mouth and fetch on command. If you are quiet and patient and *insist* that the dog pay attention, he will fetch. His option is inattention and correction. Remember, you correct for inattention.

Week Five or Six

1. Put the dog on a down and kneel in front of him.
2. Hold the object in front of his nose and say "Fetch." When he does, praise, get up and say "Come" as you back up a few steps. Have him sit. Take the object and reward him. Repeat six times.
3. Each session put the object closer to the ground, until it is on the ground. Repeat Step 2.
4. When it is on the ground you may have to pull gently on his collar with the leash to move him toward the object. Do not hurry. The key to success is that he cannot go anywhere or do anything until he picks it up.
5. When he is picking it up and bringing it to you when you stand in front of him, start throwing it very short distances. At first go with him, point to the ground and say "Fetch." When he gets the idea, take the leash off and throw the object short distances and say "Fetch." When he can accomplish the short retrieves, *gradually* lengthen them.

JUMPING HEIGHTS

Jumping heights improperly has caused many a fine dog to retire prematurely. Unfortunately, teaching incorrect methods to newcomers has generally

Jumping Table
Beginning Heights

The following height spread (determined by measuring the dog at the top of the withers), relative to the beginning height of the jumps, should be used to start all breeds. Once started, each graduation for dogs under fourteen inches should be in one-inch increments and for dogs over fourteen inches, in two-inch increments.

Dog Height at Top of Withers	Jump Height
8"—9"	2"
9"—10"	3"
10"—12"	4"
12"—14"	5"
14"—16"	6"
16"—20"	8"
20"—24"	10"

Note: Jumps should be raised each week until your dog is jumping the required height. Different organizations require different heights. Check with the rules of the club or association in which your dog will compete.

been the cause of the problem. Not physically preparing the dog properly and not giving the dog the time to prepare himself mentally are the major mistakes commonly made. Generally a dog is rushed over the jump, and this is something he is happy to do when the jump is at a height that is not intimidating to him. When the jump is raised higher, however, he may clutch up mentally and bunch up physically and this causes him to hit the jump.

Teaching your dog to jump properly is easy as long as you take one step at a time and completely follow through on each step.

1. Look at the scale in the Jumping Table to determine the height and rate of advance at which your dog will be comfortable jumping.
2. Start the dog by sitting him on one side of the jump, very close to the jump—not with just his front legs, but with his whole body. In fact, his chest should extend *over* the jump.
3. Stand six feet away on the other side of the jump and, with no leash or with an entirely loose leash, count to five or ten (be sure the dog is completely

1. Starting the pick up from the down position makes it easier for your dog.

2. Encourage your dog warmly when he starts a real pick up, but don't get too exuberant or he may drop it.

3. Coax the dog up quietly after he picks up the dumbbell.

124

4. Make sure your dog holds the dumbbell all the way to you and sits with it before you take it from him.

1. Start with your dog so close to the jump that his chest is over it.

2. Keep the dog right at the jump until the top of the jump is on a line with the point of your dog's breastbone.

3. When the jump goes above the breastbone, place your dog back one standing body length.

126

4. When the jump is level with your dog's head when he is sitting, place your dog back two standing body lengths.

5. If you follow the jump program, your dog will jump comfortably and confidently.

relaxed); say, "Jump," quietly, and back up as the dog comes over. The first few times the dog may be a little clumsy or may even just step over the jump. That is fine. Make him sit for a count of five when he gets to you. Keep quiet and keep him quiet. Let him alone to think. Don't rush him. After each count of five, praise warmly, but not with excessive excitement. It is very important to have the dog relaxed. You don't want him thinking the jump is all that important; if you attach significant importance to the jump, so will the dog and that can cause problems.

4. Repeat five times. Do the exercise at this height six times, twice a day. If you are sitting the dog where he should be, you will notice that he will not lean forward to jump but will immediately lift his front legs up. This accomplishes two things very important physically to the dog: (1) since there has been no pressure on the front for takeoff, the muscles are relaxed and the dog will land on relaxed muscles; (2) the liftoff pressure will come entirely from the back feet, legs, thighs and hips, thus giving the conditioning necessary for a high, springy, rounded jump. And, because you are allowing the dog seven days of jumping at one low height, he will have no fear of jumping. (If you miss a day—*add* one. Do not cheat!)

5. Follow the schedule for raising the jumps and moving your dog back. A body length refers to a "standing body" length.

6. For those of you who have dogs who will need to carry a dumbbell over the jump, wait until the dog is fetching well and then lower the jump to the first height and repeat the program with the dumbbell. If you have a dog that has been improperly conditioned, restart him from the lowest jump and double each allotted time. Do not use the dumbbell until the dog jumps his full height comfortably and then start all the way down again.

JUMPING DISTANCES

Jumping distances is easier for a dog than jumping heights because in this action a dog's body need only be raised a few inches off the ground by its forward motion. This is really just an elongation of the galloping stride.

1. Take a couple of flat one-inch by eight-inch by five-foot boards and raise them off the ground about four to six inches and place them four inches apart. (With a very small dog, use only one board to start). Show the dog the boards.

2. Put your dog on lead and start about eight feet from the jump.

3. Say "Jump" and then run to and jump over the boards with the dog. Repeat three times.

4. Put your dog on a stand or sit eight feet from the boards. Take his leash off. Give him the stay command and walk to the other side of the boards.

5. Touch the boards and say "Jump" as you back up quickly. The dog will jump the boards and come straight to you. Repeat three times.
6. As the days go by, *slowly* increase the number of boards and the distance between them until it is uncomfortable for him to jump any farther.

DIRECTIONS

How to give directions to the dog for going away from you is covered in Chapter 3, p. 47, under the "Go" heading. To direct the dog when he is away from you:

1. Leave him on a sit-stay and let him watch as you place two objects he knows approximately twenty-five feet apart, about twenty-five feet in front of him. These can be objects you want fetched, jumps you want jumped or small boards where you want him to stop.
2. Go back to the dog and praise him for waiting. Give a second command to stay and walk directly away from him until you are about ten feet past the objects.
3. Count to ten slowly, then give a third stay command, raise your left arm slowly and point to the object on your left. Slowly walk to it, staying in back of it by about ten feet.
4. When you get behind the object, command "Left" and "Come." When he nears the object tell him to fetch or jump or sit or down or stand (whatever you have set up). If it is a fetch or jump, as soon as he has fetched or jumped, back up to the point where you started the "Left, come" command, stop, and have the dog sit in front of you. Wait for a slow count of five. Praise and release.
5. Repeat two times to the left, and then do the same exercise to the right. Always remember to count to ten before sending the dog. This prevents him from anticipating and makes him wait for direction.
6. As he learns what you want, drop the "come" part of the "Left, come" or "Right, come" command and use only the directional command. Also, drop the "Fetch" or "Jump" command. Each day you do this exercise, instead of walking all the way in back of the left or right object, stop six inches short and one foot back from the last place you stopped. Soon you will be able to stand still, fifty or sixty feet in a straight line from your dog, and give him directions.

When your dog thoroughly understands both "Go" and the directions, you may combine the exercises. If you also teach "Open It," "Close It" and "Put It In," you will have a dog that can *go* to the refrigerator, *open* the door, *fetch* a soda, *close* the door, bring the soda to you, and when you are done, *go* to the wastebasket and *put it in!*

FIND MINE

"Find Mine" is a fun and useful exercise. It is easy to teach, since the dog already knows your scent and just has to realize that yours is what you want him to find. (If you throw a stick you have been carrying or he has been carrying into several other sticks, nine times out of ten he will fetch the one with your scent—try it.)

1. Start with dissimilar objects to make it really easy. Use a salad tong to place a few unscented objects—a bottle, small box or old book, for example—on the ground.
2. Take the dog's favorite toy or dummy, hold it for a few seconds, tell him "Stay" and put the scented object among the unscented objects. Return to the dog and tell him "Fetch" or "Find mine." He should fetch his toy. If he does not, when he comes back to you, just send him again. Do not take the incorrect object out of his mouth (if you do he may just grab another one and you want him to *smell*). After a few tries he will bring you the right one. When he does, give him a treat.
3. As he learns what you want, place more similar objects out, until they are all alike. Always be patient. When he realizes he must fetch yours (or he will be repeatedly sent out), he will try harder and eventually take the time to do it right.
4. If you are in obedience and are used to using a tie-down mat or board, try putting your unscented articles on top of each other in an "X." At first put four articles out in two X's about ten inches from each other. Place your scented article between and a little in front or back of the X's. Most dogs will avoid the X's and take the single article. If yours does not, put some hydrogen peroxide on the X's—metal only. Send the dog again. After a few tries he will bring back the right article. Use only these five metal articles at first, for one week. If the dog is accurate for a week, then slowly separate the X's. Stick with metal for three to four weeks, then repeat the same exercises with just leather—for another three to four weeks. Then combine leather and metal, but go back to the X's. Slowly spread the articles apart as the dog learns, and slowly add more articles. You will be surprised at how fast this process goes, and there is no need to worry about taking the dog off the board.

HAND SIGNALS

Hand signals are useful for a variety of reasons and are excellent in getting the dog to really pay attention to you. If you start with the four basic commands—down, sit, stand and come—you can create signals for whatever else you want. Often in movie and commercial work hand signals are required.

If you can command that kind of attention from your dog you will have come a long way from his early days in your home.

Down

Stand in front of your dog. Hold the leash in your left hand and loop it under your left foot. Simultaneously say "Down" and raise your right arm straight up (for field dogs, swing your arm down). If your dog goes down, praise quietly (remain standing in place) for five seconds, return to heel position, stand for another five seconds, release and praise. If he does not go down, pull the lead up under your foot with your left hand. This draws the dog straight down. *Do not allow any creeping forward.* Repeat once more. The third time, say nothing, just give the hand signal. If he was watching, he will go down; if not, he gets a correction from your foot on the leash. Try again. Soon he will watch and go down on signal.

Sit

Put your dog in a down. Stand immediately in front of him with the leash in your right hand. Give the dog's name and simultaneously raise your left arm straight to the left from your left side and take a quick half-step back with your left foot. This will start to bring the dog up. As soon as he starts up, simultaneously swing your left arm toward him under the lead and step toward him with your left foot and say "Sit." Praise quickly and count to five. Return to heel position, count to five again. Praise and release. Repeat a second time. The third time, drop the verbal command and execute the signal and steps only. As he learns, slowly increase your distance from the dog. If he tries to creep toward you, use a one-inch by five-foot board and sit him in back of it when you bring him from a down to a sit.

Stand

Put your dog in heel position. Start forward slowly, off leash. With a treat in your right hand, stop on your right foot and put your right hand immediately in front of the dog's nose and your left foot under his body. Do not turn toward the dog. Do not "lead" the dog forward with your right hand. Make sure he stops at your right hand. Command "Stay." Count to five and walk around him. Count to five again. Praise and release. About every third stand start using your right hand without the bait. Slowly drop all other help and use just the right hand to make the signal.

Come

Put your leash on the dog and put the dog in heel position. Leave him on a sit and go to the end of your leash. Put your leash in your right hand and

Keep your leash and foot in position to make necessary corrections should the dog fail to comply with your signal.

Step back on one foot to just start the dog up from a down position.

132

As the dog starts up, move your foot and hand forward to stop the dog from standing.

Slip your hand under the leash to help your dog complete the sit position.

stretch your hand and arm out as an extension of the leash. Give the come command and snap your right hand to your left shoulder. When he gets to you have him do a front, count to five, release and praise. As he learns, drop the verbal "Come" and just snap your right hand to your left shoulder. When he is reliable at six feet, try him on a long line. When he is reliable on a long line, go back to six feet, but without a leash. Slowly increase the distance between you and your dog. Always praise him when he comes to you.

PAW IT

"Paw It" is simple to teach because dogs naturally like to use their paws. Some dogs are almost catlike in their ability to gather or hold objects (including you!).

1. Put your dog on a down and sit on the floor facing him, a piece of food in each of your hands.
2. Show him the food in one hand and allow him to take it.
3. Let him smell your other hand, but hold the food and tell him "Paw it!" He will sniff your hand several times, then move a paw toward your hand. When he does, open your hand and let him get the treat. Repeat until you can hold your hand out, say "Paw it!" and he does.
4. Let the dog watch you put a treat under a lightweight plastic bowl. Tell him to "Paw it." When he does he will automatically get the treat!
5. When your dog gets the idea of pawing, you can have him use his feet to turn things off and on, open doors that are not latched, fetch something that has rolled under a low buffet or teach him the "shell game"—and when you are sure he understands, make a few bets with your friends!

PULL IT

"Pull It," once learned, can be used for anything from pulling a pant leg to opening a door. It is a big confidence builder for more reluctant dogs, as they can always accomplish something. Be sure your dog understands "Fetch" thoroughly, then:

1. Tie a sock or cord onto a small cupboard door that opens easily. Let the dog watch as you open the door and put a treat inside.
2. Close the door, hold the sock or cord and command your dog to fetch. As he begins to pull, open the door for him and immediately show him the treat and let him have it.
3. Repeat four or five times.
4. Next, let him pull the door open himself and get the treat.
5. As the dog gets good at opening the door, shorten the sock or cord until

Obedience classes allow your dog to gain social graces with other people and other dogs.

you can replace it with a short piece of tape. Pretty soon he will simply grab the handle. Remember, once you teach him this trick, whatever is in your cupboards is fair game!

OBEDIENCE CLASSES

Socialization is very important in strengthening the stability and dependability of your dog's actions and reactions. Good obedience classes give you an excellent opportunity to accustom your dog to working among other dogs and people and to receive professional direction at the same time. Be cautious in selecting your training school. Be sure the instructors are experienced and are teaching in a manner you are comfortable with. Abuse of animals should never be tolerated. For every legitimate trainer there are probably a thousand who are not. A good trainer will keep you from making mistakes and show you how to keep your dog's attitude positive while he learns. If the dogs you see are accurate in their work and have happy, tail-wagging attitudes, you have probably found a good school.

OBEDIENCE RULES AND REGULATIONS

If you wish to compete in obedience trials you will need to know the rules. You can write to the American Kennel Club or the United Kennel Club for rule books. It is a good idea to attend obedience classes that include competitive instruction. While the rule books are explicit, it usually takes a long time to really understand the terminology, and a good class will help immensely. If you have a mixed breed dog, you can compete at unsanctioned matches. The rules will be the same, but your degrees will come from another association. See Chapter 7, "Obedience Competition."

9

Table Manners for Show Dogs

BUYING AN ADULT SHOW DOG rather than a promising puppy has many advantages. Most important is that you know what you are getting in structure and basic temperament. The dog is probably well socialized and conditioned for a positive attitude—perhaps a little too positive in some cases. If you are reading this before purchasing a dog, you should be aware of a few general facts.

1. Breeders usually do not sell their best dogs, and if they do it is usually not to a novice. If they do sell their best to a novice, it is usually with strings attached. Make sure you are willing to live with those strings before you buy.
2. Price does not guarantee quality. This is definitely a "buyer beware" market. Attend several dog shows in your area and talk to the people who have purchased from local breeders. Ask their advice. A reputable breeder will price his dogs fairly. A good breeder will not only be fair, but will also go out of his way to help you get a good start.
3. Contrary to what you may hear ringside (from the losers), most dog show judges are reputable and honest. If they were not, we would not have literally hundreds of novice owners just from our own center who have personally finished the championships on their dogs. But these novices have paid their dues and have spent many class hours learning to be "professional." They have done their homework in learning what judge is likely

to put up the type of dog they have. And they do not show their dogs before the dogs are ready. Showing dogs is a great sport, and while it is not for everyone there is simply nothing like putting a championship on a dog yourself, unless it's putting one on a dog you have bred.

CONTRACTS

When a show-quality dog is purchased, there should always be a written contract between the buyer and seller. The problem in buying your first show dog is that you often do not have enough information to know what must be included in the contract. The following issues must be addressed:

1. Request a health provision that guarantees normalcy in the hips, elbows and eyes; no blood deficiencies; no inherited diseases particular to the breed that are life endangering or will restrict breeding capabilities; no breed disqualifications or faults so severe as to effect a condition that would make it impossible or highly improbable to finish the dog's championship.
2. If a co-ownership is involved, be exact as to the rights and responsibilities of both owner and co-owner.
3. Be specific about whether there will be a replacement of the dog or a refunding of money if the contract becomes void. Note who takes control of the dog in question.
4. If the purchase includes a "puppy-back package," be specific as to which puppies in which litters (for example, seller gets choice of first and third puppy from first litter).

ADAPTING A KENNEL-RAISED DOG TO YOUR HOUSE

Housebreaking is generally the worst problem you will face when buying a kennel-raised show dog and bringing him into your home. At the kennel these dogs are free to eliminate whenever they wish. They often mark and remark their pen, as the dog's mark next to them activates this natural tendency. If you already have a dog in the house, this problem is going to require a lot of attention and time. It is important that you set the rules from the moment the dog enters the house—not only for him, but as a reminder to all other animals living therein.

1. Keep the dog on a leash for at least two weeks, tied to you.
2. Take him out for frequent walks or turn him loose frequently in your backyard.
3. Make sure he is crated or penned at night or tied up short to your bed.
4. Follow the advice on housebreaking in Chapter 6.

138

ADAPTING TO A TRAINED SHOW DOG

Adapting to a trained show dog can be an unnerving experience if all that has ever been done with the dog is to take him from a kennel or crate, put him in an exercise area, groom him and show him. I have had new clients of two- or three-year-old show dogs come to me and say, "He is really beautiful, but boy, is he stupid—he can't even fetch a ball!" He isn't really stupid. It is just that many breeders do not have time to play with all their dogs. Many breeders want to save all their dog's energy for the show ring, so no one has ever bothered to use that dog's brain. The new owner must indoctrinate the dog to "home life."

1. Keep your dog leashed for a long time, because if he gets away he will have no idea how to return.
2. Agility training is one of the best ways I have found to start a "stupid" dog thinking. Basic agility can be handled on leash, and since the training is all food- and praise-oriented, no corrections are involved. Agility physically and mentally stimulates the dog.
3. Try helping the dog do something he was bred for, such as fetching if he has a hunting background or herding a ball or livestock if he has a herding background. If you have the time or are inclined to do something other than show the dog in breed competition, try taking part in some of the other activities available to your dog.
4. Take lots of walks in different places and watch him come alive as new smells and sights excite him. If he has fears, do not contribute to them by trying to placate or soothe him. Just stand or sit calmly and wait until he relaxes. If you are not afraid and if you ignore the problem, so will he.
5. Try some basic obedience training. Get help from a good instructor who knows how to condition a dog in several areas. Do not let your breeder tell you "you can't do both." (Our walls are full of pictures—over three hundred—of dogs that have titles in more than one field.)

CONDITIONING AN UNTRAINED SHOW DOG

Conditioning an untrained show dog can take a lot of patience, but the results of your work are very rewarding. Untrained show dogs are usually kennel-raised and do not have the benefit of all the hands-on socialization that the "best puppies" got.

1. Socialization with strangers is first on your list after the break-in time at his new home (a few weeks). Choose a good training center with positive trainers who are used to handling show dogs.
2. If there is no such center near you, take the dog for walks around shopping

centers and spend as many hours a day as you can just allowing strangers to pet your dog.

3. When the dog is relaxed under the Step 2 activities, find some informal matches to go to or set up one with some of your friends who are in the same situation. Go over each other's dogs like a dog show judge would.

4. Get a good book on conformation handling (ask a breeder or at your pet shop) and practice the suggested routines. Books that describe your own breed and how to best handle these dogs are most helpful.

5. Several times before the dog's first show, wear exactly what you will be wearing in the ring. This helps relax not only the dog, but you as well. You will be sure the pockets are where you need them and that the shoes do not hurt your feet.

PHYSICAL CONDITIONING

Good physical condition must be maintained for all show dogs. Proper exercise is essential for good muscle, proper weight and fluidity of movement. Many times, if a show dog is not being campaigned, he is left in the kennel too much. If this is the case, go jogging or biking with your dog. This will help the bonding process as well as the physical conditioning.

1. Start slowly. Some dogs that have been kenneled too long, especially large growing puppies, have little or no muscle tone. In such cases, just walking, sitting and getting up may dominate your schedule for several weeks.

2. As the dog seems more comfortable with the exercise, extend the distance and speed (walk, then jog, then slow trot, then extended trot). Most good conditioning comes through long jogging, not a faster gait.

3. Take heart, and work. A proper diet, proper exercise and plenty of love can do wonders.

KEEPING COAT

Keeping the coat on a show dog in show condition can be relatively easy if you have a Dalmatian or Doberman but can be very time consuming if you have a terrier that must be stripped or a large rough-coated breed like the Chow Chow or Old English Sheepdog. A well-kept coat is often the difference between obtaining the points and walking out without them. So often the words heard from judge to steward are, "Too bad he wasn't in coat. I liked his type and he moved well." Breeders often put so much emphasis on coats that they become huge and burdensome, and unless they are well taken care of, they can cause health problems. So, care must be taken:

1. The coat and skin should be kept clean and free of parasites. The coat should be brushed every few days and combed regularly to avoid matting

and to remove all dead hair. Your breeder or groomer can show you what needs to be done to keep your particular dog's coat in the condition dictated by the breed standard. If you keep the coat well groomed, when show time arrives you will have only to perform some last-minute brushing, bathing and trimming.

2. Teeth should be clean, too. There is nothing more disgusting than opening a mouth and finding plaque-caked teeth, sore or bleeding gums and bad breath. Brush the dog's teeth daily.
3. Toenails should be cut back so that you hear no clicking on the floor. Be sure to cut dewclaws, if your dog has them.
4. Ears and feet should be trimmed or plucked in accordance with the breed and need. Most show dogs are accustomed to this grooming, but if you need help, talk to the breeders in your area.

LEARNING THE RULES

Pamphlets containing the rules for dog show competition are available from the American Kennel Club, 51 Madison Avenue, New York, New York 10010. To a newcomer these rules may seem very confusing. Often the best way to educate yourself to their meaning is to get a rule book and take it to a show. Sit next to the experienced fanciers at ringside and ask them for help. They will teach you what classes are in the ring and in what order, and they will help you learn about reading the catalogue so you can follow along with the judging.

OBSERVING DOG SHOWS

While at an all-breed show you will also be able to watch a variety of events.

1. When you enter the show look for the grooming areas. It is fascinating to watch the dogs' final preparations. This is also a good place to meet breed people. If you see a particular dog you like and if the handler or owner does not have time to talk to you, ask for a card so you can call him later.
2. Walk around the show area and look at the booths. Everything a dog could possibly need will be sold at the shows, as well as note cards, jewelry, stationery, art, T-shirts, books and tents.
3. Walk around the rings and look at all the different breeds. It really is simply amazing! If you stay for the Group and Best in Show competition, you can see the best of each breed, according to the judges that day.
4. In the obedience rings you can watch handlers and their dogs perform individual and group exercises that demonstrate the usefulness of the dog and his willingness to participate in public events.

Students spend many hours practicing to make sure they and their dogs look like pros.

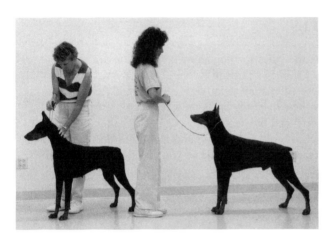

It is necessary to teach your dog hand stacking and free stacking as they both are needed in the ring.

Dogs must learn to stand for examination without showing fear or aggression.

142

5. Find the sponsoring club's show table and see if any special events are going to be held. Many clubs feature the AKC's breed tapes, which usually run all day. Some hold flyball or scent hurdle races; some hold agility exhibitions; some weight pulling, and so forth. If a particular breed is having a supported entry, there may be a featured event geared toward that breed.
6. Be sure to buy a catalogue and write notes and questions. Take it home and if all your questions were not answered at the show, you will have literally hundreds of names to call upon.

LEARNING JUDGES' PREFERENCES

Every judge will have a personal preference as to the type of dog he believes best. Until you have developed an eye for a good dog yourself, it will be difficult for you to evaluate different judging styles. There are basically two types of judges: breeder/judges, who start in one or two breeds and whose successful breeding careers lead to judging; and all-rounders, who generally come up via the route of professional handling. While all-rounders may also be breeders, they generally have had more involvement with a greater variety of breeds and variety of types within the breeds and may put somewhat more emphasis on balance and movement than type (type, in essence, is head, coat and tail). If you can recognize the type a certain breeder/judge is placing you can be pretty sure he will almost always stick to that type if given the choice. All-rounders also demand type in their winners but may recognize more than one type as having value. The balance of the judging differences is good for the sport as a whole. It ensures type with soundness and balance.

LEARNING TECHNIQUE

There are four basic patterns used when moving your dog. See Chapter 4, p. 56, for a discussion of these patterns. Also, attend conformation classes and observe handlers at matches and shows. Practice walking with your dog and looking over your left shoulder at your dog's tail. This helps *you* attain a "professional gait" to help minimize your presence in the ring and maximize your dog's presence.

To show your dog to his best advantage, you will need to learn how to free stack and hand stack your dog (see Chapter 4, pp. 52–54). Also, remember that the most important technique you can develop in hand stacking is to keep your dog's head up and in one place—not only as you hand stack him, but also as you move out of the hand stack to either bait him or move him. *Always* keep control of your dog's head.

This handler practices with one of her own champions. She sometimes chooses to handle her own dogs and sometimes hires a handler. Knowing how to show herself enables her to choose competent handlers.

Always remember that your show dog is really just an everyday dog that happens to be beautiful!

OWNER HANDLING VERSUS HIRING A HANDLER

Whether you show your dog yourself or hire a professional handler depends on your objectives and priorities. It often takes an owner/handler longer to finish his dog, but the pride you gain by doing so is worth the effort—as is the knowledge you gain by handling your own dog. Once you have finished a dog, you are in a better position to evaluate whether you enjoyed it enough to do it again. If not, at least you are in a better position to choose a handler.

10

Teaching Tricks for Pleasure, Conditioning and Possible Profit

W HATEVER the future you have chosen for your everyday dog, the conditioning you have accomplished by now should have instilled all the necessary ingredients to enable your dog to learn to put two and two together. He should be attentive, social, happy and willing. Take advantage of your hard work. Pick out the exercises in this chapter that appeal to you and have some fun. Every exercise will not only enhance your relationship with your dog, but also continue to instill good, steady behavior.

Many of the exercises test your dog's basic temperament. If there are still some lingering problems, perhaps they can be ironed out here. Does your dog still retain some submissive characteristics? Work on the exercises listed under "Tricks from the Stand or While Moving." Is he still somewhat aggressive? Work on the exercises listed under "Tricks from the Down." Is he absolutely wonderful, and do you just want to have a really good time and entertain for fun—and perhaps for profit? Work on everything! And certainly do not limit yourself to these. From these you should be able to figure out how to help your everyday dog do anything he is capable of doing. Just use your imagination.

his Irish Setter regally offers his paw to shake ands.

If he can shake, he can wave.

A pretty sit up from a pretty girl!

TRICKS FROM THE SIT

Shake Hands

1. Teach either "Shake Hands: One" or "Shake Hands: Two" from Chapter 5.
2. Have your friends begin to shake hands with your dog.

Wave

1. Teach "Wave," from Chapter 5.
2. Teach your dog the hand signal for wave by eliminating the verbal command every other time you reach out for his paw (and do not take it).
3. As he learns the signal, stop bending over and just reach your hand toward him and gesture as a maestro would when asking for a little more forte!

Sit Up

1. Put your dog in a sit and stand directly in front of him.
2. Take a treat and hold it directly above his head.
3. When he reaches up, make him stretch his nose up toward the bait. When he does reward him with the bait.
4. Each time you hold the bait up, have him stretch farther. Increase the stretch slowly and start telling him "Sit up."
5. When his feet begin to come off the ground, hold the bait steady at that point so he can learn to balance himself. If you move the bait too high, too soon, it will throw him off balance.
6. As he learns to balance himself more securely, tell him "Stay" and make him hold the position for a few seconds. As he learns, gradually start moving back.

Speak

1. Teach "Speak," from Chapter 5.
2. Add a hand signal by closing your right thumb to your right fingers rapidly, fingers pointed toward the dog. When he will respond by speaking at the signal only, teach him to change tones.
3. Move your fingers and thumb close together between their opening and closing and whisper the command. After a while he will speak softly.
4. Use a normal voice and signal for a normal bark.
5. Use a very wide open-and-close motion and an excited tone to your voice when you give the "Speak" command and this will bring the bark out loudly and sharply.

Prayers can be done on your arm or a piece of furniture or on the floor itself.

6. The whisper can also be converted to a low growl—when you want this. Use the same hand signal, but say "Growl" softly and slowly.

Say Your Prayers

A picture is worth a thousand words, no matter what your beliefs!

1. Have your dog sit at your left side.
2. Put your left arm in front of his body, just underneath his breastbone.
3. Tap your arm with your right fingers and tell him "Shake" or "Paw it."
4. As soon as he puts his right paw on your arm lift your arm up slowly so that his other paw comes up, too. When both paws are on your arm, tell him to stay.
5. Take a treat and with your right hand, lead his nose down between your arm and his chest and say "Prayers."
6. When his head is positioned so that his eyes are hidden by your arm, give him the treat. As he learns, you can substitute a chair or bed for his paws to rest on.

TRICKS FROM THE DOWN

Play Dead

1. Teach "Play Dead," from Chapter 5.
2. Teach the hand signal by giving the command verbally and simultaneously turning one arm, held at waist level, out in front of you, from a palm-down position to your side in a palm-up position.
3. Repeat until you can give the signal alone.

Roll Over

1. Teach your dog "Play Dead" and have him die.
2. Teach "Roll Over," from Chapter 5.
3. Teach the hand signal by giving the verbal command and simultaneously using your right or left hand, palm down, to make a small circular motion over the dog's head. Repeat until he will roll over on a hand signal alone.

Roll Up in a Blanket

This trick contains three commands the dog must already know—down, fetch and roll over.

1. Put a large, soft blanket on the floor (at least three times as large as your dog).
2. Put the dog in a down on the blanket, near to and facing one corner of the blanket.

1. To play dead right takes a lot of character.

2. Lady capitulates slowly to her demise. . .

3. . . . and carefully lowers her head. . .

4. . . . and dies. . . so well!

3. Take a corner from the left or right of him and give it to him with the command "Fetch." Caution him gently to hold it.
4. Use both verbal and hand signals and tell him "Roll over." He will be confused at first and may drop the blanket several times. Just be patient. When he does understand what you want, change the command to "Roll up."

This is a fun command to use when you have guests, have had a fun evening but are really ready for them to leave. Just say to your dog, "Why don't you get your blanket and roll up for the night?" When the dog wanders off, gets his blanket, brings it back and rolls up in it, he is saying to your guests "Good night!"

Crawl

1. Teach "Crawl," from Chapter 5.
2. Increase your distance from the dog as he learns what you want and gets secure in the command. Move back slowly. If the dog tends to stand up, use a fishing pole or some other long, thin tube to hold over the dog's back. Tap him lightly if he starts to get up when he should be crawling.
3. Teach him to crawl up and down stairs.
4. Teach him to crawl, then play dead.

Head Down

1. Put the dog in a down-stay.
2. Hold a treat in one hand, directly in front of his nose, and tap the floor with your other hand, just below his nose.
3. Give the command "Head down" and slowly move the hand with the bait down to the floor. Speak slowly and softly. When his head just reaches the floor, quietly say "Stay" and hold still until he gets tired and his head actually rests on the floor. Praise quietly, wait five seconds, then release and reward him.
4. Head down can be used in any position (for example, when sitting—head down to a table or chair).

TRICKS FROM THE STAND OR WHILE MOVING

Close the Door

1. Take your dog to a door that you have opened just an inch or so and stand him in front of it.
2. Take a soft treat that is a little sticky in your left hand and place it about

Head down can show a variety of expressions. This Aussie's soulful stare goes right for the heart!

1. Tabby can open her crate door. . .

2. . . . and put herself to bed.

153

a foot above his head *against* the door (sort of stick it on the door). Take your right hand and pat above your left hand and say "Close it."

3. As your dog reaches up to get the treat, one or both front feet will touch the door. At that instant, help him shut the door and praise effusively and reward him immediately.
4. Repeat with the door open just a little bit more until he is actually pushing the door closed without being afraid of the sound or weight of the door.
5. As he becomes secure in what he is doing, stand back a little, point to the cheese on the door and command "Close it." He should be eager to try for the cheese and will stand there on his hind legs and eat it after he has closed the door.
6. Gradually leave the cheese off and reward him *after* he has closed the door.

Turn Off/On the Light with Paw

1. If you have switches on the wall or at the base of a lamp that can physically be worked fairly easily with your hand, the dog can work them with his paw. Teach "Paw It" from this section first.
2. Take the dog to the switch and put your hand next to the switch. Pat that area and tell your dog "Paw it." Keep tapping your hand until his paw hits the switch. As soon as the light goes on or off, praise and reward. This is easy to teach once the dog realizes that the light changes from on to off (he may do it later for his own amusement!).
3. When he understands what you want, change the command to "Turn it off" or "Turn it on."

Turn Off/On the Light with Mouth

1. Make sure your lamps will not be pulled over when the dog pulls on the cord. Teach your dog "Pull It" from Chapter 8.
2. Show your dog the cord you want pulled and say "Pull it." When he does and the light goes on or off, reward him.
3. When he learns what you want, change the command to "Turn it off" or "Turn it on."

Go to "John"

1. Teach "Go," from Chapter 3.
2. Start teaching your dog the name that goes with each person you want him to go to ("John," "Dad," "Mom" and so forth) by having him go to each person for one week before starting on another person's name. Always use the person's name. It also helps if the dog knows how to fetch and can carry one certain item to that certain person. For instance, have him carry "Dad's slipper to Dad." As kids, we used to have our dogs carry messages from one house to another. Whatever house the dog was sent to always had a

Instead of running for your phone, teach your dog to get it and then take it back and hang it up.

dog biscuit ready to reward the "carrier," so the dogs were always eager to go!

Put It In

1. Teach "Fetch," from Chapter 8, first. Place an open box with sides that reach about to your dog's elbows on the floor.
2. Tell him to fetch an object that can easily fit into the box.
3. As he goes to fetch the object, place yourself on the far side of the box and put a treat in your hand.
4. As he returns and reaches the opposite side of the box, direct your treat and hand down into the box and say "Put it in." When he drops the object in the box, give him the reward. If he misses, make him fetch again and try again. Do not give him the reward until he hits the box.
5. When he understands "Put it in," sit in a chair near the box and throw something for him. Have him fetch it and when he brings it back, point to the box and command "Put it in." When he understands, start putting the command to use—for putting kids' socks in hampers, empty cans in waste-baskets, toys in toy boxes and so forth. Dogs love to use their mouths, and this is a good way to use them constructively.

Answer the Phone

1. Teach "Fetch," from Chapter 8, first. Place some adhesive tape on the handle of your phone's receiver and take it off the hook.
2. Take your dog to the phone and tell him "Fetch the phone." When he does, have him give it to you and praise him.
3. Repeat until he is used to having the phone receiver in his mouth and he will not drop it until it is securely delivered to your hand.
4. Place the receiver across the phone, but not actually in place, and tell the dog "Fetch the phone." Work at this until he gets the receiver and delivers it to you. Lots of praise!
5. Place the receiver in the phone where it belongs and have the dog repeat Step 4 until he can do it all himself. Then, change the command to "Answer it."
6. Arrange for a friend to help one day. Have him ring you on the phone and tell the dog to answer it. Pretty soon he will answer a ringing phone on his own. If you want to have some fun, teach him to speak after he has answered it.

Hang It Up

1. Place the phone on a table that is about chest high for your dog and sit your dog facing the phone. Get on the other side of the table and face your dog.
2. Take the receiver off the phone and tell your dog "Fetch." Have him hold the receiver for four or five seconds.

3. Pick the phone base up and put it under your dog's chin and tell him "Put it in" or "Give" or "Drop it" (whatever release word you have been using). If necessary, *gently* open his mouth so that the receiver will drop out. At first this is hard for the dog to understand, so be patient.

4. When he will drop the receiver on command, put the phone back on the table and have him repeat Step 3 until he understands that he is to drop it on the phone on the table.

5. Start requiring accuracy in the drop before giving praise or a reward. If it is not accurate, make him fetch again and try again. He will soon understand, and once he does, he will *always* get it in right.

6. Now you are ready to have him handle the phone from start to finish. When it rings, have him answer it and bring it to you. When you are done talking, have him hang it up. This is one of our favorite public demonstrations, as people can hardly believe their eyes when they see dogs, from a Miniature Schnauzer to a Siberian Husky, answering and hanging up phones.

Take It to "John"

1. Teach "Fetch" and "Go," both from Chapter 8.
2. Put them together.

Open It

1. Teach "Pull It," from Chapter 8.
2. Tie a cord to a drawer that slides easily and put a treat in the drawer.
3. Take your dog to the cord and tell him "Pull it." When he does, show him what is in the drawer.
4. It takes only a few minutes to teach this trick. When your dog understands it, if he knows "Fetch," you can have him open a drawer and fetch things from it for you.
5. As he understands what you want, change the command to "Open it" and shorten the cord, until you are up to the drawer handle. Wrap the cord around the handle and have him open the drawer with the handle. Soon you can remove the cord completely.
6. Start teaching him to open other drawers by using the same method. But realize that you are opening your entire house to the dog.

Find My Money

This is a great game. You can use it to win some bets.

1. Teach "Fetch" first, and then "Find Mine," both from Chapter 8.
2. Take two fresh dollar bills that you have not touched and put them on the ground a few inches apart using a pair of tongs.
3. Take a dollar bill from your wallet, hold it in your hands for several

seconds, and crumple it up a little bit. Place it a few inches from the other two.

4. Show your dog the money, then take him about ten feet away from the money. Wait, let him look at it for a few seconds (develop his curiosity), then tell him "Fetch" or "Find mine."
5. He should bring the right one back. If he does, praise and reward him. If he makes a mistake, just send him back. Do not take the money from his mouth. Let him put it down and pick up the right dollar. When he does, lots of praise.
6. When you are *sure* he understands, have a friend scent the two other dollars. Put yours out there and send your dog to fetch. If he is successful, have your friend scent two more dollars. When you are totally confident of his ability, take someone who has not watched this training process and bet them your dog can find his own dollar among their four other dollars. If you win, fine. If you lose (your dog can make a mistake—he is canine after all), just go back and do some more work. Never get upset. If you do the dog will get nervous and you may never win.

Puzzle Board

This is an advanced trick and you should try it after you and your dog have real understanding and real communication going. It takes lots of patience, but when you complete it, you can really feel proud and your dog will, too, as he will know he has done something special. You must first teach "Fetch" (Chapter 8), "Paw It" (Chapter 8), and "Put It In" (this chapter).

1. Make a board one inch deep by twelve inches wide by three feet long. Trace four shapes: circle, triangle, square and cross, each about eight inches in diameter, onto the board and carefully cut them out. Take a one-eighth-inch piece of particle board, cut twelve inches wide by three feet long and put it on one side of the board for a backing. Paint the board white. Cut a quarter inch off all sides of the cut-out shapes and paint each shape a different color.
2. Put the board on a table about chest high to your dog.
3. Put the circle shape on the ground and have your dog fetch it, saying "Fetch the circle." Have him bring it to one side of the board while you kneel in front of the other side facing him.
4. Move the board so that the cut-out for the circle is under his chin and tell him "Put it in." If, when he drops it, it goes into the circle space, praise and reward. If it just drops on the board, tell him "Paw it" and tap the circle shape until he tries to paw it. Help him move the shape into place. He will hear the little click as it falls into place and that will help him understand what you want. Work on just the circle until he understands. This may take a week or two of working for a few minutes every day.
5. When he understands how to get the circle in, start on the square—then

the triangle, then the cross. Be sure to name each piece. He will eventually connect the name with the place on the board and realize that only one name fits in each place. When the two of you have mastered this trick, you should treat each other to a steak!

Go Hide

First teach "Down," "Go," and "Pull It," from Chapters 3 and 8.

1. Get a suitcase with stiff sides, large enough to allow your dog to lie down and curl up in it.
2. With the lid up, place a treat in a back corner of the suitcase. Tell the dog "Go hide" and let him walk into the suitcase to get the treat. Once he has it, tell him "Down." Wait five seconds, release and praise him. Repeat six times.
3. On the seventh try, after he is down, lower the lid for just a second. Repeat until the dog can stay there for twenty to thirty seconds without fear.
4. Attach a small tie line to the inside center of the top of the suitcase. Send the dog into the case and give him time to lie down, then tell him "Pull it" and show him the line. Coax him to take the line and at first help him pull the top closed. Repeat until he can close it himself.
5. If the top of the suitcase is soft, let it rest on the bottom. Once the dog can stay inside, have him "nose" his way in (to get the treat) and then tell him "Down."
6. From this trick, you can have your dog "Go hide" in boxes, cupboards and so forth.

Scratch Yourself

1. Every time you see your dog scratch, make the same motion with your hand on your body and say "Scratch, good boy. Scratch."
2. Put some double-sided tape on the inside of your dog's collar. When it catches some of his hairs he will try to scratch it off. At that moment tell him "Scratch." (Then take the tape out.)
3. At odd times, stick a small piece of tape to the back of the hair on the back of his ear with a thread pressed under the tape. The combination of the tape and thread may make him scratch; if so, say "Scratch." (Then take the tape off.)
4. Be sure to use the same motion he is using when you command "Scratch," as this will help him learn faster.

Dance

1. Put a treat at the end of a six-foot piece of quarter-inch dowel.
2. Hold the treat just above the dog's head and say "Dance." Get him excited

and as soon as he reaches for the treat give it to him. Each time you put a new piece of treat on the stick, raise it a little, until he must stand up to get the treat.
3. Repeat until he can dance for several seconds.
4. As he learns, use your arm and hand to point up above his head and command "Dance."

Wag Your Tail

1. Look at your dog and say "Wag your tail" in the same tone as, but quieter than, you would say "Do you want a cookie?" Say it again. By the second or third time, he should wag his tail.
2. As soon as the tail wags, go get a treat. Do not start with a treat and do not praise afterward, as this gets him too excited and much more than his tail will wag.

Stop

This is an extremely handy command for any dog to know—for obvious reasons.

1. Have your dog stand in front of you, then tell him "Stay" and back up about six feet.
2. Put a four-foot, quarter-inch dowel in your right hand and point it to the floor.
3. Quietly call the dog and when he gets halfway to you say "Stop" and move forward, sliding the stick *quietly* toward him on the floor. You do not want him jumping sideways, away from the stick. You just want him to stop.
4. When he stops, say "Stay," count to ten, praise and release him. Repeat six times.
5. As he learns, make the distance between you and your dog farther apart when you start. Eventually you will be able to stop him anywhere.

Jumping into Your Arms

Jumping into your arms is fun and can be done from the floor or from ladders, big rocks and so forth.

1. Start by placing the dog on a step of a stair.
2. Place his front paws on your chest and happily say "Jump." Lean back and snatch him up to you.
3. As he learns to come forward into your chest, stay an inch or two from him, just pat your chest, say "Jump" and encourage him to jump toward you. Be sure to catch him!
4. When he can jump from a stair to you, try from a chair, then the floor, then any object you want. Again, make sure you always catch him.

Make sure you are fast enough to catch the dog—otherwise, he may not want to jump again.

SPECIAL NEEDS

Posing for Pictures

Whether you are posing for print or moving shots, you will always have times when the dog needs to remain basically motionless for long periods of time, then raise or lower his head or turn it slowly from side to side so that the director can get the angle he is looking for. This is tedious work for you and the dog so be very patient and use a lot of treats to get started.

1. Start with the dog in a sit (then repeat from the down and stand). Stand about two feet in front of your dog and hold a treat at his eye level and tell him "Watch." Count to ten and give him a treat. Give the "Watch" command again and move your hand slowly an inch to the right, count to ten, and reward. Repeat to the left. Repeat up and down. Always start center and then work right, left, up and down.
2. Increase the count time until the dog will hold basically still for ten to fifteen minutes.

Rest

Learn to take a rest *before* your dog needs it. If you do not rest, the dog will quit on you. Do not let yourself be pushed by anyone to overwork your dog. Directors and producers often think that dogs are machines. It is up to you to protect your dog. Rests should include potty breaks, short walks and sleeping time.

Hands Off, Everyone!

If you get a modeling job for your dog, make sure this is the first rule you make everyone follow. The only exception is for an actor who needs to work with the dog. Do not be tempted to let anyone else pet the dog until all the work is totally over. Professional industry people know this is an accepted rule—but a cute dog is hard to resist. The dog will have plenty to do just adjusting to cameras, lighting and scores of people stepping over and running around him—all while he is supposed to be paying absolute attention to his "lines" (so to speak).

Transferring the Dog to the Actor

1. Get the actor and the dog together informally—take a walk. After a few minutes have the actor lead the dog and give him some treats.
2. Send the dog to the actor several times from ten to twenty feet away. Always have the actor reward the dog.
3. Rehearse away from the set until you work out what the script or story-

1. Slight changes in the position of the head are important to directors and photographers.

2. Lighting aids can help contain or produce shadows, but without them posing alone makes the picture.

1. "Look right."

3. "Look here." Tabby has worked in print, movie and live media and has learned to ignore commotion of every kind in order to concentrate on her handler's orders.

2. "Look left."

boards call for. Most directors are not aware of what you need to do to get the dog to do what they want. If you work it out first, it will be easier for everyone. Most actors are willing to cooperate, as the dog's actions will affect their scene, too.

Ignoring Everything

Doing commercial media work is exciting. Most of us want to be stars of some kind, even if it comes through being the owner of a dog star. When you first find yourself the center of attention it is awfully hard to ignore the "bright lights." But you will soon find out that the glamorous world painted in pictures is a very small part of the real world and that lots of hard work goes into media productions.

Patience is not an art. It is a necessity. Contracts involving working hours are mostly ignored once they have been signed and eighteen-hour days are commonplace. Dressing rooms *may* be provided for the stars, but you will often find even the stars perched on tables or sitting under trees, sweltering from the heat or freezing from the cold. Your dog will get no better conditions and much of his comfort is up to you. Take everything you need for him to each location and make sure he will be comfortable working with any necessary props, as well as the lights, cameras, various noises and so forth. Ignore everything that is not absolutely necessary for the work you are doing. You will have enough to do just making those conditions the best possible.

Afterword

THE PRECEDING CHAPTERS have given you some guidelines for conditioning and training your dog to adapt to your lifestyle. The amount of time you take and the consistency with which you approach the training will, to a great degree, determine your success.

The methods used herein are certainly not the only ones that can be used to attain success. But patience, persistence and praise are mandatory. The key to your success throughout remains the same: physically stopping the dog from doing what you don't approve until his attention is registered on you and then, and only then, showing him what you want.

I am consistently impressed and entertained by the creativity of my clients and have learned never to say "You can't do it that way" because usually they already have! For instance, when Lynn Feilmeier decided her Sheltie, Shawna, should have learned how to fetch the dumbbell consistently and still did not, Lynn took one evening, a broom and two pounds of Cheddar cheese to solve the problem. If Shawna fetched on command she was rewarded with the cheese; if she did not, Lynn swatted her with the broom! Lynn was very persistent, and when Shawna realized she had only two choices, she took the one attached to the cheese!

Liz Frisbee has Siberian Huskies. Liz is unable to make a correction that involves any degree of pain to her dogs. And yet, while not the best of "obedience" dogs per se, one of them is one of our most trusted and versatile movie and commercial dogs. She can set a table or clear it; answer a phone or hang it up; open a cupboard, take out any item, bring it to you and, when you are finished with it, put it back or throw it into a wastebasket; she can open

166

Whether posing for a head study. . .

. . or giving us a happy face, this everyday dog
can do it all!

a chest, jump in and pull the lid down; play basketball; get a big blanket off the bed and roll up in it; and perform all the "usual" tricks—speak, play dead, crawl and so forth. How does Liz teach her? With food rewards. And the more difficult the trick, the better the reward. When Liz first told me, "Nahanee won't do that trick for cheese, that needs liver," I was a little skeptical, but I needn't have been. Once the reward is bargained, the dog performs!

Betty Cantor's two Standard Poodle boys once thought about creating some "games" for themselves when Betty went to work. So, she started calling her answering machine and leaving them messages. Her last message tells them when she is coming home. The result—no more games and Crete and Le Beau are always waiting to greet her at the garage door.

Florence Kantor also expresses "mind over matter" in dealing with her eight male house dogs (two Standard Poodles, four Lhasa Apsos, and two Silky Terriers). When asked how she makes them all get along she answers, demurely, "Easily, I'm head bitch!"

One more set of instructions:

1. Allow yourself the luxury of spending a few minutes alone with your dog each day.
2. Believe you will be successful in making your dog the perfect image of what you want him to be, but remember he is just a dog.
3. Clear everything from your mind when you work with your dog and concentrate solely on what you want him to learn.
4. Do give your dog the benefit of the doubt.
5. Eliminate negative force training and implement simple physical stops until you have your dog's attention.
6. Finally, have fun with your dog! Allow him to entertain you. Take spontaneous walks and have an occasional ice cream cone together. Laugh with your dog. Such times will bring you both great joy.